Social Media Investigation for Law Enforcement

Social Media Investigation for Law Enforcement

Joshua Brunty
Katherine Helenek

Series Editor
Larry S. Miller

AMSTERDAM • BOSTON • HEIDELBERG • LONDON
NEW YORK • OXFORD • PARIS • SAN DIEGO
SAN FRANCISCO • SINGAPORE • SYDNEY • TOKYO
Anderson Publishing is an imprint of Elsevier

Anderson Publishing is an imprint of Elsevier
The Boulevard, Langford Lane, Kidlington, Oxford, OX5 1GB, UK
225 Wyman Street, Waltham, MA 02451, USA

First published 2013

Notices
Knowledge and best practice in this field are constantly changing. As new research and experience broaden our understanding, changes in research methods, professional practices, or medical treatment may become necessary.

Practitioners and researchers must always rely on their own experience and knowledge in evaluating and using any information, methods, compounds, or experiments described herein. In using such information or methods they should be mindful of their own safety and the safety of others, including parties for whom they have a professional responsibility.

To the fullest extent of the law, neither the Publisher nor the authors, contributors, or editors, assume any liability for any injury and/or damage to persons or property as a matter of products liability, negligence or otherwise, or from any use or operation of any methods, products, instructions, or ideas contained in the material herein.

British Library Cataloguing-in-Publication Data
A catalogue record for this book is available from the British Library

Library of Congress Cataloging-in-Publication Data
A catalog record for this book is available from the Library of Congress

ISBN: 978-1-4557-3135-0

For information on all Anderson Publishing publications
visit our website at store.elsevier.com

This book has been manufactured using Print On Demand technology. Each copy is produced to order and is limited to black ink. The online version of this book will show color figures where appropriate.

CONTENTS

A MESSAGE FROM THE AUTHORS

We were approached to write this book after we presented our research entitled "Facebook: Do You Leave a Trace? A Forensic Analysis of Facebook Artifacts" at the American Academy of Forensic Sciences (AAFS) conference. Attendees of the presentation were interested in the traces and forensic artifacts that Facebook left behind for investigators to uncover and use in their investigations. Many were quite surprised at the fact that anything posted not only onto Facebook but also to other social media sites, cannot truly be deleted and is discoverable by law enforcement.

After much discussion between ourselves, we decided it was our responsibility as academics and law enforcement supporters to take on this unique project and make an easy-to-read yet thorough and informative text regarding social media and law enforcement investigation.

In this book, we address the different categories of social media sites and their functions, along with how such sites can be exploited and abused. The many different uses of social media by law enforcement are explained, and the legal issues that already exist or would arise in the future are addressed. In addition, this text provides direction to commonly asked questions in the law enforcement community, such as how to capture and obtain social media evidence, and the tools and resources available to assist in such a unique investigation.

We hope you find this book both informative and entertaining, while gaining new knowledge regarding social media and law enforcement. We want you to be aware of the effects of social media while questioning and evaluating certain legal decisions regarding the First Amendment issues of free speech and Fourth Amendment issues of search and seizure. In addition, we hope this text provides the sources you need to continue your education on this subject if you find it interesting and wish to pursue a career path in digital forensics and/or investigations.

Lastly, take away safety tips about protecting yourself, your family, and your friends on the Internet. Social media sites can be a great and exciting way to keep in touch with colleagues, friends and family, meet new people, learn about new movies and books, share photographs and discover new places and ideas. However, as professionals in this field it is important to take the proper precautions and keep yourself informed, and we hope this book will help you become a safe and smart social media user.

Sincerely,

Josh Brunty and Kathy Helenek

ACKNOWLEDGEMENTS

Thank you to Jad Saliba, CEO of Magnet Forensics for providing high-resolution images for inclusion into the text.

– Joshua Brunty

I would like to thank Wes Gibson for his guidance and support during the writing of this text. I very much appreciate the time he took to read over and edit chapters, along with his artistic improvements to my graphics.

– Kathy Helenek

CHAPTER 1

Introduction to Social Media

When we think about social media, a few things immediately come to mind: Facebook, friends, games, Twitter, Internet, iPhone. We are all familiar with social media in one form or another. Television shows advertise their Facebook page containing games and program information. News stations broadcast opinionated Tweets from Twitter regarding current events. Businesses connect with customers through foursquare so that fans can receive deals and companies may advertise to a specific audience. There are many popular social media sites today which vary in their uses, all the way from fundraising for charities to creating a centralized database of information, from CouchSurfing.org, which lets members find places to stay while traveling, to partyflock.nl, a Dutch community for people interested in house music. Although we are all familiar with what is considered social media, many are unfamiliar with the definition of social media and what exactly differentiates social media from other forms of media.

1.1 DEFINITION OF SOCIAL MEDIA

According to Boyd and Ellison (2007), social networking sites are "web-based services that allow individuals to (1) construct a public or semi-public profile within a bounded system, (2) articulate a list of other users with whom they share a connection and (3) view and traverse their list of connections and those made by others within the system" (p. 211).

By breaking down this definition and building on it, we can define what exactly constitutes social media. A social medium allows the user to create a profile within the site; this may consist of a personal picture, screen name, e-mail address, avatar, symbol or other depiction. The profile gives users a specific and unique identification so that other members may identify him from all other members on the system. Once users have created a unique profile, they may find and connect with other members on the site. This includes friends or acquaintances from the real world, and may extend to users met through the site itself.

Once the user has connected with others on the site, it may be possible to see not only his own connections made through the site but connections that other members have also made within the system. Viewing of other member's connections depends on how the social site is designed and what privacy settings users have enabled.

Building on Boyd and Ellison's definition, we can further define social media. A social medium (4) encourages its users to communicate with other users who are a part of that network and/or the site creators themselves, and (5) creates an environment for users to share content and/or connect through their similar interests. Many social media sites offer different ways for users to communicate with one other: instant messaging, e-mailing, real-time video or voice chatting. One of the goals and thus a characteristic of a social medium is a sense of community among users. Members of a site are able to distribute and share their content with one another, or may be able to unite through similar interests and hobbies.

1.2 A VERY BRIEF HISTORY OF SOCIAL NETWORKING

Ever played the game "Six Degrees of Kevin Bacon?" A random individual is chosen and the players try to make a connection from the selected person to actor Kevin Bacon in six links or less. As arbitrary as the number six seems for this game, it actually comes from a scientific theory. An Italian inventor, Guglielmo Marconi, through his research and experiments of wireless telegraphy, postulated that any two people throughout the world should be linked by a chain of 5.83 intermediaries or less (Hayes, 2000).

According to Boyd and Ellison's definition along with our own additions, the first social network was SixDegrees.com, originally launched in 1997. The idea behind SixDegrees was to promote social associations and business contacts. A user became part of the network by filling out the information form and listing ten e-mail addresses of associates. Contacts were ordered by degrees, so one was able to see his first-degree contacts, second-degree contacts, eventually leading to the sixth degree, which included the entire SixDegrees.com network. It consisted of electronic bulletin boards, e-mailing and online messaging. There was also an internal search engine which allowed users to search and find others with similar interests (Bedell, 1998). It was the first web site to combine successful features from other popular sites to create

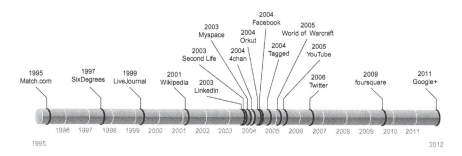

Fig. 1.1. Social media timeline.

a social network. It also included profiles, which were normal on dating or community sites, buddy lists from chat programs and networks that high schools and colleges commonly used, such as Classmates.com (Boyd and Ellison, 2007) (Fig. 1.1).

As the Internet continues to expand and improve, social media sites develop and grow as well, attempting to reach high popularity among users and attract more participants. This growth continues in the present, where social media sites are an everyday part of our lives.

1.3 TYPES OF SOCIAL MEDIA

There is currently a wide variety of social media available on the Internet, each designed for different purposes. Some sites promote an environment for all users, while others create a place for people with specific and/or similar interests. Social media sites have been categorized to explain their uses and purposes in a descriptive manner. These categories include collaborative projects, blogs and microblogs, location-based, content communities, social networking sites, virtual game worlds, virtual social worlds and dating sites (Kaplan and Haenlein, 2010). Many of the different types of social media sites will synchronize with one another so users can interact through multiple social media interfaces simultaneously.

1.3.1 Collaborative Projects

Collaborative projects encourage users to contribute to the content of the site. All users are essentially writers, editors and proofreaders; any member can be involved in the project to help assist in the final outcome of the collaboration.

1.3.1.1 Wikipedia

Wikipedia is a free-content online encyclopedia project, where any user may add information to subject pages in order to increase the knowledge database. Articles are continually created and updated, allowing users to have up-to-date written and stored information about events in a matter of minutes rather than weeks or years. Each article contains links which cross-reference additional articles about an associated subject. These connected articles allow users to quickly find related information regarding a specific subject. Since any user may update an article, there are concerns regarding accuracy; many errors may be found in the encyclopedia. Wikipedia states that "the ideal Wikipedia article is well-written, balanced, neutral and encyclopedic, containing comprehensive, notable, verifiable knowledge." Pages and articles are actually edited, discussed and debated among users, eventually taking on a neutral point of view reached through a general consensus ("Wikipedia: About," n.d.).

1.3.2 Blogs and Microblogs

The term "blog" comes from Jorn Barger who, in 1997, published a series of links in reverse chronological order, naming it Robot Wisdom WebLog. Users started referring to other sites containing posts in reverse chronological order as WebLogs as well. An online journalist then split the word "WebLog" into "We Blog," coining the use of the common term "blog." Microblogging developed a few years later, consisting of smaller and shorter blog posts (Carvin, 2007).

Blogs and microblogs give users a chance to express their personal thoughts and opinions on a wide variety of subject matters. The textual content varies from both nonfictional and fictional articles to journal entries and short stories; content often includes streaming video, audio and photographs. A very popular microblog these days is Twitter.

1.3.2.1 Twitter

Twitter is a web site which allows users to post on a real-time information network. The community is open to everyone from all demographics, and is often used by celebrities; it is a place where members connect to the latest stories, ideas, opinions, and news. Each post is known as a Tweet, which is 140 characters long at the most ("About Twitter," n.d.). By March 2012, Twitter's sixth birthday, more than 340 million tweets were posted each day – that is more than one billion tweets every three days (@twitter, 2012).

1.3.3 Location-Based

Location-based social media sites and applications allow users to tag their geographical location. Members can check into specific stores, helping businesses advertise, distribute coupons and attract more customers.

1.3.3.1 Foursquare

Foursquare is a popular example of a location-based social medium. Users "check in" at a location, which lets them discover what specials are offered along with other possible attractions nearby. Businesses commonly place coupons and deals on foursquare, giving members the opportunity to save money and hopefully inspire their friends to join them. A certain competitive aspect exists on the site, making the user who checks in the most at a single location the "mayor" of the check-in point. If another user checks in more times than the current mayor, he can be ousted from office and a new mayor is then declared ("About foursquare," n.d.).

1.3.4 Content Communities

Content communities are social media sites that allow users to share all different types of content with one another. This may include photographs, articles, short stories, videos, games and presentations.

1.3.4.1 YouTube

YouTube was founded in February 2005 and lets users watch and share videos ("About YouTube," n.d.). YouTube's vision is to give every member a voice and support the evolution of video. As of June 2012, forty-eight hours', or two days', worth of video is uploaded each minute, resulting in nearly eight years of content uploaded every day ("Frequently," n.d.). The following site automatically displays the most popular videos (n.d.) from different categories on YouTube: http://www.youtube.com/topic/4qRk91tndwg/most-popular.

1.3.4.2 4chan

4chan originally started as a project founded by the administrator "moot." It is an image-based bulletin board where users post comments and share images about all different topics, which has been growing ever since its development. The site wants users to contribute by adding images and posting comments to the boards which are substantial, helpful, friendly and humorous ("4chan," n.d.).

1.3.5 Social Networking Sites

Social networking sites are probably the most well-known type of social media. Facebook is a household name that is now anywhere and everywhere. Social networks require users to create a profile with a variety of content and then connect with other members. The key difference between a social medium and a social network comes down to the fact that social networks focus on the relations between members. Ties and connections between users add together and expand to create a social network. It then becomes possible to identify certain groups and subsets of members, along with the strength of specific relationships according to the types of exchanges, frequency of contact, intimacy or duration of connections (Haythornthwaite, 2005, p. 127).

1.3.5.1 Facebook

Facebook lets users simply and easily sign up to become members, create profiles and then connect with friends and acquaintances. The profile normally consists of a profile picture, contact information, photographs, statuses, work, education, interests, hobbies and friends.

Members can stay in contact with friends and family, discover what is happening in the world, and share and express what matters to them. Facebook offers a variety of interfaces in which to communicate with other friends: timeline, activity log, news feed, photos, video, groups, messages, events, subscribe, ticker and pages (Press@fb.com, n.d.a). Facebook reported 901 million active users monthly as of the end of March 2012, about 80% of which were located outside of the United States and Canada (Press@fb.com, n.d.b).

The Social Network (2010), a popular movie released in 2010, chronicles the creation and development of Facebook by Harvard student Mark Zuckerberg. A trailer for the movie can be found here: http://www.youtube.com/watch?v=lB95KLmpLR4. The film reveals many of the issues that transpired during the site's launch; the many problems that occurred during the start-up may surprise members who are unaware of the history of Facebook.

1.3.5.2 LinkedIn

LinkedIn is a social networking site aimed at professionals who would like to make contacts and display their work experience. This form of social networking is coined "professional networking," the virtual counterpart of conventions or trade group meetings. Many members use the site to find and apply for jobs or to let others know their qualifications and capabilities. As of March 31, 2012, LinkedIn was the largest professional network with 161 million members in over 200 countries and territories. Hundreds of thousands of job applications have been submitted using the site. LinkedIn even has executives from all of the Fortune 500 companies as members on the network (About us, n.d.). The following article demonstrates how important LinkedIn and social media are for job recruiters looking for candidates: http://news.cnet.com/8301-1023_3-57469282-93/heads-up-linkedin-users-93-of-recruiters-are-looking-at-you/.

1.3.6 Virtual Game Worlds

Virtual Game Worlds are three-dimensional environments where players are represented by avatars. Massively Multiplayer Online Role-Playing Games (MMORPG) are made up of thousands of players in the same game interacting with one another. They must play while connected to the Internet, and there are specific rules members must abide by within each environment.

1.3.6.1 World of Warcraft

World of Warcraft is an MMORPG that occurs in a fantasy universe created over fifteen years of previous Warcraft games. Each character has a specific set of skills which defines that user's role in the game. Gameplay involves fighting monsters and completing missions, either individually or as a team of online players. There are hundreds of hours of gameplay available for the World of Warcraft members ("What is World of Warcraft," n.d.). A funny viral video exists which actually takes place in the World of Warcraft universe: http://www.youtube.com/watch?v=L5Jni6isNSE.

1.3.7 Virtual Social Worlds

Virtual Social Worlds are very similar to Virtual Game Worlds; both allow the user to create an avatar and interact with other members in a virtual environment. However, Virtual Social Worlds are not as constrained by the rules of a game, allowing users to intermingle much more freely.

1.3.7.1 Second Life

Second Life is a three-dimensional community where an avatar represents a user. Every object in the environment is constructed and placed by the Second Life members. You can "enter a world with infinite possibilities and live a life without boundaries, guided only by your imagination." By becoming a member, users design the physical appearance and clothes of their 3-D avatar, and then may explore the Second Life world. Members can visit new places and meet new people. Direct communication between users is achieved using voice over Internet protocol (IP) or text through the site ("What is Second Life," n.d.).

Linden Lab, based in California, sets up the computer servers for Second Life and auctions out pieces of undeveloped land in the game. Developers can then come along and buy this land (US currency can actually be converted to "Linden dollars"), transforming it however they desire; some add rivers, houses, gardens, clubs – the possibilities are endless. Some Second Life users choose to buy these renovated properties from developers in order to build up their own personal accounts (Sloan, 2005). In 2006, Anshe Chung, a developer and seller of property in Second Life, became the first millionaire of a virtual world (in US dollars): http://www.businessweek.com/the_thread/techbeat/archives/2006/11/second_lifes_fi.html.

Second Life has, in some cases, permeated into the real world, affecting peoples' lives in reality. Marriage, cheating, engagements and divorces are some of the events that have occurred in the virtual world and have unfortunately occurred in actuality as well. Here is an interesting article about a couple who went through their own unique ups and downs over their Second Life accounts: http://www.dailymail.co.uk/news/article-1085412/Revealed-The-woman-Second-Life-divorce--whos-engaged-web-cheat-shes-met.html.

1.3.8 Dating Sites

It has become fairly common for Internet users to meet future partners or significant others through online dating sites. The term "dating" is used loosely in this categorization, referring to the interaction or contact with future sexual partners, activity partners or marriage/union partners. Many of these sites promise the use of a meticulous matching algorithm in order for users to meet their best possible matches; others simply promise a large number of users so members may browse through a wide variety of profiles. A multitude of sites exist as well for users of all different tastes and appeals, ranging from sugardaddie.com to muslimfriends.com.

Critics have questioned the credibility of certain dating sites' abilities to connect users on a romantic level. eHarmony claims to match users with someone who has been "prescreened for deep compatibility with you across 29 dimensions." Due to the nature of connecting through cyberspace, these sites are unable to take into account the variables that occur when two people meet one another, such as communication patterns, problem-solving tendencies, and sexual inclinations. Studies have shown that the way in which couples discuss and solve disagreements predicts their future satisfaction and whether or not the relationship will last or fall apart. As dating sites might claim to have a high compatibility factor, the true determinant of a relationship will occur once two people meet in person (Finkel and Karney, 2012).

1.3.8.1 Match.com

Match.com is a dating web site where users pay to meet people and plan dates with the hopes of finding a significant other. Users first create a profile, in which they tell about themselves and what qualities they're looking for in another person. Members then can search for other Match.com users based on their interests, background, age and location. Every day, the site will send members personalized matches. Once users find someone they are interested in, they can send a wink, an e-mail or chat on Instant messaging (IM) ("How it works," n.d.).

1.4 SOCIAL SOFTWARE BUILDING BLOCKS

Many people have studied social software and attempted to determine exactly how social media functions and how the interaction between people operates on these sites. Butterfield (2003) came up with an original list of five characteristics consisting of Identity, Presence, Relationships, Conversations and Groups. Webb (2004) further expanded upon qualities by adding Reputation and Sharing. Smith (2007) reviewed the seven mechanisms and created a social software honeycomb. Identity is placed in the center of the honeycomb, since it is the most basic requirement of any social media system; the remaining six factors make up the outside of the honeycomb (Fig. 1.2).

Kietzmann, Hermkens, McCarthy and Silvestre (2011) provide thorough definitions for each of the functional building blocks of social media.

1.4.1 Identity

Identity is how the member is represented and recognized on the site by other users. This may be a username, avatar, profile, photo or any other factor that may give the user his/her unique identity on the site.

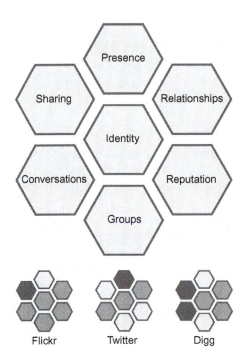

Fig. 1.2. Social honeycomb diagram. Image used with the permission of Smith (2007).

1.4.2 Presence

Presence is the awareness of members sharing the same site with one another. It lets users know the availability of other members such as active, busy, idle or other statuses the site may offer.

1.4.3 Relationships

Relationships are simply how the members relate to one another through the social medium. Sites may have different terminology for connections but have the same general idea of visualizing a user's contacts. Relationships have been called friends, buddies and contacts, just to name a few.

1.4.4 Conversations

Conversations are the means through which members can communicate with one another on the site. Depending on the site, different options may be available. Some social media have instant messaging or e-mailing, while others may offer video or voice chatting.

1.4.5 Groups

Groups allow members to join and become part of a unit with others on the site for a common purpose. Users can form their own communities and feel like they belong to a unique group.

1.4.6 Reputation

Reputation is the ability for members to identify the standing of others. This can be in safety terms, such as seeing a warning level a user has received, or popularity terms, as in a rating level. Some sites offer the option to "like" or rank the content other members have posted.

1.4.7 Sharing

Sharing content is one of the largest aims of social media. Members are able to post their personal thoughts, opinions, ideas, questions, feelings, links, videos, photographs, pictures or whatever types of media the site supports. Sharing on social media sites allows users to exchange, distribute and receive content.

1.5 ACCESSING SOCIAL MEDIA

For almost a decade, the Internet could only be accessed through a computer, but technology is rapidly changing. Desktop and laptop computers are no longer the only devices used to browse the Internet. It is now possible to access the Internet from almost anywhere with the use of wireless access or cellular networks. A plethora of new technological devices allow users to connect to the Internet, such as cellular phones, tablet computers and video game systems.

1.5.1 Cellular Phones

It is has been estimated that mobile phone Internet users will outnumber desktop Internet users around 2014 (Meeker, Devitt & Wu, 2010). As of April 2012, 88% of US adults own a cell phone. More than half of these cell phone owners use their phones to browse online due to the convenience and availability of a mobile phone. 17% of cellular phone users state they primarily go online using only their phone and not another device such as a laptop or computer (Smith, 2012) (Fig. 1.3).

Fig. 1.3. Smartphone users in the world. Image used with the permission of http://www.go-gulf.com/ – web design company.

1.5.2 Tablets

Tablets have been on the rise since they first appeared to the public. Tablets are small portable touchscreen computers which allow access to the Internet. They can contain music players, streaming capabilities, face-to-face video chats, cameras, global positioning system (GPS) units and e-Readers. Just like computers, tablets vary in their size, speed, memory and processing power ("Tablets," n.d.). 19% of adults in the United States now own and use a tablet (Rainie, 2012). Businesses are starting to incorporate the use of tablet devices into their daily workflow. Some companies have even developed Bring Your Own Device (BYOD) to work policies (Toksal, 2012).

1.5.3 Video Game Systems

56% of homes in the United States currently own a seventh generation gaming console. Game systems let users browse the Internet as well as interact via multiplayer games; watching videos on-demand and streaming services on game consoles are also increasing in use (Hopkins, Pike & Pollack, 2012). According to a Nielsen report on US Gaming, consoles are the most common way users play games. 86% of teens engage in gaming on a console such as the Xbox, PlayStation or the Wii, all of which can be connected to the Internet. Many of these game consoles have as much processing power as a personal computer (Lenhart et al., 2008).

1.6 CONCLUSION

A social media site can be defined as such by its basic intentions and associations. Sites have been improving the interfaces and features of social media for years; applications are constantly being developed and added each day to keep sites appealing and interesting for users. Many different categories of sites make up what is known as "social media"; however, many of these sites share similar characteristics and common objectives. It is important to understand the basic mechanisms of successful social media sites in order to recognize and investigate how members can be deceived, exploited and manipulated. Keep in mind the technological devices discussed in this chapter used to access social media, and be aware of new products that will be introduced to users in the future.

REFERENCES

@twitter, (March 21, 2012). Twitter turns six. *Blog* Retrieved June 18, 2012, from <http://blog. twitter.com/2012/03/twitter-turns-six.html>.

2012 Best Tablet Side-by-side comparisons and reviews. (n.d.). *TopTenREVIEWS*. Retrieved June 20, 2012, from <http://tablets-review.toptenreviews.com/>.

4chan – Frequently asked questions. (n.d.). *4chan*. Retrieved June 27, 2012, from <http://www.4chan.org/faq>.

About foursquare. (n.d.). *Foursquare*. Retrieved June 19, 2012, from <https://foursquare.com/about/>.

About Twitter. (n.d.). *Twitter*. Retrieved June 18, 2012, from <https://twitter.com/about>.

About us. (n.d.). *LinkedIn Press Center*. Retrieved June 19, 2012, from <http://press.linkedin.com/ about>.

About YouTube. (n.d.). *YouTube*. Retrieved June 18, 2012, from <http://www.youtube.com/t/ about_youtube>.

Bedell, D. (October 27, 1998). Meeting your new best friends: Six Degrees widens your contacts in exchange for sampling web sites. *The Dallas Morning News*. Retrieved June 4, 2012, from <http:// www.dougbedell.com/sixdegrees1.html>.

Boyd, D. and Ellison, N. (2007). Social network sites: Definition, history, and scholarship. *Journal of Computer-Mediated Communication*, *13*(1), 210–230. Retrieved June 4, 2012, from <http://ezproxy.marshall.edu:3344/doi/10.1111/j.1083-6101.2007.00393.x/pdf>.

Butterfield, S. (March 24, 2003). An article complaining about "social software" and a rebuttal from Ross Mayfield. *Sylloge* (Retrieved June 20, 2012, from <www.sylloge.com/ personal/2003_03_01_s.html#91273866>).

Carvin, A. (December 24, 2007). Timeline: The life of the blog. *NPR* Retrieved August 14, 2012, from <http://www.npr.org/templates/story/story.php?storyId=17421022>.

Finkel, E. and Karney, B. (February 11, 2012). The dubious science of online dating. *The New York Times* Retrieved August 27, 2012, from <http://www.nytimes.com/2012/02/12/opinion/sunday/online-dating-sites-dont-match-hype.html?_r = 1>.

Frequently asked questions. (n.d.). *YouTube*. Retrieved June 18, 2012, from <http://www.youtube. com/t/faq>.

Hayes, B. (January–February, 2000). Graph theory in practice: Part I. *American Scientist*, *88*(1), 9–13. Retrieved June 4, 2012, from <http://www.cs.uc.edu/~annexste/Courses/cs690/hayesgraphpart1.pdf>.

Haythornthwaite, C. (2005). Social networks and internet connectivity effects. *Information, Community & Society*, *8*(2), 125–147. Retrieved May 30, 2012, from <http://dx.doi.org/10.1080/13691180500>.

Hof, R. (November 26, 2006). Second Life's first millionaire. *Businessweek* Retrieved August 16, 2012, from <http://www.businessweek.com/the_thread/techbeat/archives/2006/11/second_lifes_fi.html>.

Hopkins, B., Pike, N. and Pollack, C. (February 7, 2012). US gaming: A 360 view. *Nielsen* Retrieved June 21, 2012, from <www.nielsen.com/content/dam/corporate/us/en/reports-downloads/2012-Webinars/US-Gaming-A-360-View.pdf>.

How it works. (n.d.). *Match.com*. Retrieved August 27, 2012, from <http://www.match.com/howit-works/index.aspx?lid=4>.

Kaplan, A. and Haenlein, M. (2010). Users of the world, unite! The challenges and opportunities of social media. *Business Horizons*, *53*(1), 59–68. Retrieved June 15, 2012, from <http://ac.els-cdn.com/ S0007681309001232/1-s2.0-S0007681309001232-main.pdf?_tid=2348486ebc62c63c6caf5f133bae985 0&acdnat = 1339792453_58b04c2ec441c05c2c>.

Kietzmann, J., Hermkens, K., McCarthy, I. and Silvestre, B. (2011). Social media? Get serious! Understanding the functional building blocks of social media. *Business Horizons*,

54(3), 241–251. Retrieved June 20, 2012, from <http://ac.els-cdn.com/S0007681311000061/1-s2.0-S0007681311000061-main.pdf?_tid=67f334174d4e178681aedf4e8a9ec362&acdnat=1340207834_614069afe159d87b165>.

Lenhart, A., Kahne, J., Middaugh, E., Macgill, A. R., Evans, C. and Vitak, J. (September 16, 2008). Teens, video games and civics. *Pew Internet* Retrieved June 21, 2012, from <www.pewinternet.org/~/media/Files/Reports/2008/PIP_Teens_Games_and_Civics_Report_FINAL.pdf.pdf>.

Meeker, M., Devitt, S. and Wu, L. (April 12, 2010). Internet trends. *Morgan Stanley* Retrieved June 20, 2012, from <www.morganstanley.com/institutional/techresearch/pdfs/Internet_Trends_041210.pdf>.

Most popular in all categories. (n.d.). *YouTube.* Retrieved August 14, 2012, from <http://www.youtube.com/channel/HC4qRk91tndwg>.

Press@fb.com. (n.d.a). Key facts. *Facebook Newsroom.* Retrieved June 19, 2012, from <http://newsroom.fb.com/content/default.aspx?NewsAreaId=22>.

Press@fb.com. (n.d.b). Products. *Facebook Newsroom.* Retrieved June 19, 2012, from <http://newsroom.fb.com/content/default.aspx?NewsAreaId=19>.

ProtoArmor. (February 11, 2010). Leeroy Jenkins: Censored version with subtitles 480p! *YouTube.* Retrieved August 16, 2012, from <http://www.youtube.com/watch?v=L5Jni6isNSE>.

Rainie, L. (January 23, 2012). Table and e-book reader ownership nearly double over the holiday gift-giving period. *Pew Internet* Retrieved June 20, 2012, from <www.pewinternet.org/~/media/Files/Reports/2012/Pew_Tablets%20and%20e-readers%20double%201.23.2012.pdf>.

Revealed: The "other woman" in Second Life divorce … who's now engaged to the web cheat she's never met. (November 14, 2008). *Mail Online.* Retrieved August 16, 2012, from <http://www.dailymail.co.uk/news/article-1085412/Revealed-The-woman-Second-Life-divorce--whos-engaged-web-cheat-shes-met.html>.

Sloan, P. (December 1, 2005). The virtual Rockefeller. *CNNMoney.* Retrieved August 16, 2012, from <http://money.cnn.com/magazines/business2/business2_archive/2005/12/01/8364581/index.htm?cnn=yes>.

Smartphone users around the world—Statistics and facts (Infographic). (January 2, 2012). *Go-Gulf.com.* Retrieved June 20, 2012, from <http://www.go-gulf.com/blog/smartphone>.

Smith, A. (June 26, 2012). 17% of cell phone owners do most of their online browsing on their phone, rather than a computer or other device. *Pew Internet* Retrieved June 28, 2012, from <www.pewinternet.org/~/media/Files/Reports/2012/PIP_Cell_Phone_Internet_Access.pdf>.

Smith, G. (April 4, 2007). Social software building blocks. *nForm* Retrieved June 20, 2012, from <http://nform.com/publications/social-software-building-block>.

SonyPictures. (n.d.). The Social Network official trailer—In theatres October 1, 2010. *YouTube.* Retrieved August 15, 2012, from <http://www.youtube.com/watch?v=lB95KLmpLR4>.

Toksal, A. (April 18, 2012). The year of the enterprise tablet—Infographic. *Vertic* Retrieved June 20, 2012, from <http://www.vertic.com/blog/year_of_the_enterprise_tablet_infographic/>.

Webb, M. (April 28, 2004). On social software consultancy. *Interconnected* Retrieved June 20, 2012, from <www.interconnected.org/home/2004/04/28/on_social_software>.

What is Second Life? (n.d.). *Second Life.* Retrieved June 20, 2012, from <http://secondlife.com/whatis/?lang = en-US>.

What is World of Warcraft. (n.d.). *Blizzard Entertainment, Inc.* Retrieved June 19, 2012, from <http://us.battle.net/wow/en/game/guide/>.

Whitney, L. (July 10, 2012). Heads up, LinkedIn users: 93% of recruiters are looking at you. *CNET News* Retrieved August 16, 2012, from <http://news.cnet.com/8301-1023_3-57469282-93/heads-up-linkedin-users-93-of-recruiters-are-looking-at-you/>.

Wikipedia: About. (n.d.). *Wikipedia, The Free Encyclopedia.* Retrieved June 18, 2012, from <http://en.wikipedia.org/wiki/Wikipedia:About>.

CHAPTER 2

How Social Media Is Used

2.1 HOW SOCIAL MEDIA IS COMMONLY USED

The many different uses and benefits of social media is the main reason this form of communication has become so popular. Most social sites are available at no cost and open to anyone who wishes to join. Social media is not just for keeping in touch with friends anymore; consumers, businesses and organizations have also noticed the benefits these sites offer our society today and have joined the social media revolution.

2.1.1 Personal/Consumer Use

A common reason users actively participate on social web sites is in order to keep in touch with old friends while maintaining their current relationships. Users get the chance to create profiles that portray them in the best possible light and are thus accepted by their peers. Information provided in the profiles can be very general, such as name, favorite books and types of music enjoyed. Profiles can also contain more personal information, such as political views, sexual orientation and religious beliefs (Stutzman, n.d.).

Initially, social media members used the sites to communicate and disseminate information to others, but currently these sites have added a consumer component to their base as well. Facebook users can "like" any product: television shows, movies, music, clothes, shoes, etc. There are even stores with hangers that digitally display the number of Facebook "likes" a particular clothing item has received. The fashion retailer C&A has started an initiative in Brazil called "Fashion Like"; users may go to the company's Facebook web site to like their favorite items of clothing, and the hangers in the store show the amount of likes in real-time (Byford, 2012).

Other companies have made it possible to tag photographs on social media sites with product and brand information, which, if clicked on, allows the user to directly purchase the item. The buy button is incorporated directly into the images; no searching for items or hunting through other web sites is necessary (Jonas, 2011). The Luminate site is aimed at advertisers – it explains how companies can tag their photographs to enhance the consumer's experience and promptly buy a product: http://www.luminate.com/advertiser/ ("Advertisers," n.d.).

2.1.2 Businesses

It is extremely rare these days for a business or company to not have at least one social medium describing or advertising their product. Not only have businesses discovered free advertising, but they can now publicize products to literally every part of the world. Sales and marketing personnel have realized the potential social sites hold for their companies and have studied and maximized this potential in order to sell their merchandise. Advertisers perform studies and surveys along with writing journals and articles specifically for companies to be able to maximize their use of social media in order to obtain the highest profit possible (Fig. 2.1).

McCorvey (January 25, 2010) from *Inc.* magazine describes how social networking sites can actually drive business. Just a few of his suggestions about creating a page include "making it benefit-based, talking about new or uncommon features and including some discounts and savings". Foursquare is a popular social site which promotes businesses; locations are able to claim their venue on the site, connect with possible clients who are nearby, and then offer deals and coupons to consumers to use at the store ("Foursquare," n.d.). Foursquare even offers analytics such as determining the time of day the most customers check in and the gender breakdown of those checking in ("Merchant," n.d.).

2.1.3 Organizations

Organizations, foundations and charities are also taking advantage of the far-reaching scope of social media. Certain politicians or political organizations have waged a "social media war," presenting their stances and opinions for everyone to see while bashing their opponents. Determined from a Pew Internet & American Life Project Report conducted by Aaron Smith, 21% of online adults used social networking sites to connect to the November 2010 campaigns or election, and 2% of online adults connected via Twitter. In total, 22% of adults engaged in the campaigns and elections using social media sites. Smith (2011) states "as Americans increasingly use these sites to connect with public figures, find out about and respond to events in the news, and share

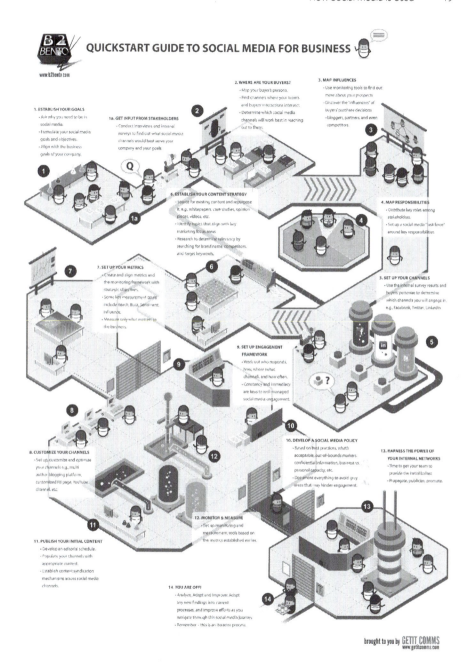

Fig. 2.1. Quickstart guide to social media for business. Image used with the permission of B2Bento.com licensed under a Creative Commons Attribution-Share Alike 3.0 Singapore License.

their views on a range of topics, politicians and political groups on both ends of the ideological spectrum have begun using them to organize and communicate with their supporters and the public at large" (p. 2) (Fig. 2.2).

Thomson (2012) reveals another side of the story, where press officers, not actually the politicians themselves, are the ones in charge of the social media accounts. Very few of the politicians who are active on social media engage and interact with their voters in a meaningful way. Many will remember Anthony Weiner and the "Weinergate" scandal. Weiner was a politician who personally ran his own Twitter account and often tweeted back and forth with his followers. Unfortunately, the married Weiner also used the account to flirt with young women. He attempted to send a picture in a private message to one woman, but accidently posted the photographs of himself in just his underwear on Twitter for the entire world to see. He claimed he was hacked, but

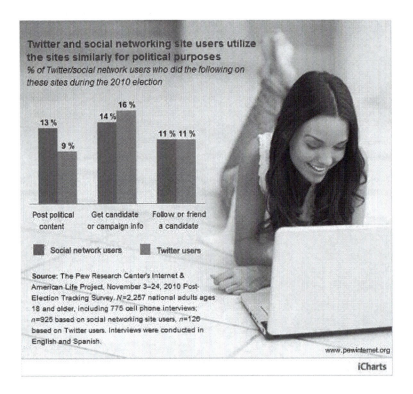

Fig. 2.2. Social media and the 2010 election. Image used with the permission of the Pew Internet & American Life Project.

resigned shortly after. Since then, many political leaders have discouraged politicians from operating their own accounts (p. 2).

Foundations and charities also use social media as a way to announce their principles and purposes to the world. Using social sites, they are able to advocate their causes, promote events and raise money. Lovejoy and Saxton (2012) analyzed exactly how nonprofit organizations use Twitter. They concluded tweets by nonprofits can be characterized into three groups: information, community and action. "We might think of informing as the basic function of Twitter; this involves spreading information about the organization, its activities or anything of potential interest to followers. The second function, 'community,' taps into how organizations can foster relationships, create networks and build communities on Twitter through tweets that promote interactivity and dialogue. The heart of this function are 'dialogic' messages and those that attempt to build a community of followers via 'bonding' messages, such as 'thank you' and acknowledgement tweets. The third function, which we call 'action,' has as a central purpose the aim of getting followers to 'do something' for the organization, whether it is to donate, buy a product, attend an event, join a movement or launch a protest." Lovejoy and Saxton (2012) believe these three functions can be applied to any nonprofit social media communications.

2.2 CRIMINAL USES OF SOCIAL MEDIA

2.2.1 Twenty-First-Century Burglary

A new serious threat has risen over the past decades – the threat of the Internet. Crime is not only a physical danger anymore; thieves may steal your information, identity, money and more without leaving their home. The connectivity and use of the Internet has created a web which leads directly between and into users' homes. Access to personal information, files, photographs or passwords are always at risk of being hacked or stolen. The Internet creates a new means for thieves, fraudsters and predators to commit traditional crimes. The Norton Cybercrime Report (2011) found that 431 million people have been the victim of cybercrime in the last year, more than the entire populations of the United States of America, Canada or Western Europe. The report also discovered "cybercrime is bigger than the global black market in marijuana, cocaine and heroin combined ($288bn) and approaching the value of all global drug trafficking ($411bn)."

Twenty-first-century burglars look to social media to help them perpetrate their crimes. Social media members often post their birth dates, which many people commonly use in passwords or personal identification numbers (PIN). Certain web sites will ask for a birth date in cases of lost passwords, aiding criminals in the quest to log-in using another person's information. The same is true for pet names and mother's maiden names – all of this supposedly harmless public information can be used against users. Just like typical robbers and fraudsters, Internet thieves have a variety of goals and crimes in mind. Some get paid to send people to sites where they will click on malicious links; others want passwords or social security numbers to steal money or identities. Certain twenty-first-century burglars want to take over social media identities, or in some cases, take complete control of Internet-connected computers (Almasy, 2009).

2.2.2 Social Engineering

Obtaining information and hacking without actually using any technical skills is known as social engineering. Social engineers simply use human interaction and conversational skills in order to obtain secrets; they use certain psychological and emotional aspects of people to their own advantage. They are expert manipulators who have perfected the art of getting others to divulge private or confidential information. The act of social engineering is not necessarily a crime in and of itself – the crime occurs when the information gathered becomes used in an illegal manner.

Hinkley (2010) describes a social engineering mission using social media: "Let's assume I am a malicious person and I want to obtain all the user account data and records for a particular organization. Their physical security is relatively good, and I have failed at high level attempts to get any kind of employee information. Let's hop on LinkedIn and do a company search for this organization. Easy enough – I now have a list of potential targets, their job titles, employment histories, education history, affiliated organizations, business contacts and in some cases their pictures. With the information here, I can narrow down a few targets based on what I am trying to find, pull up more intimate information regarding their family, friends and hobbies on Facebook and have a very specific profile on the potential targets. Armed with this information, it would be easy to spoof a text message from a business contact or spouse asking them to visit a web site containing malware and exploits. I could use their hobby information to entice them to click a link or open an attachment from a carefully crafted e-mail that allows me to plan a virus. On a more advanced level and far more nefarious level, I could build a geolocation profile from embedded location information in posts and photographs. Then all I have to do is wait for someone to work at a coffee shop and step away from their briefcase for a moment to slip in a USB drive loaded with auto-executable binaries that they'll eventually plug in to a computer" (Fig. 2.3).

One of the most infamous social engineers is Kevin Mitnick. Mitnick was caught and arrested by the FBI in 1995 for breaking into the Fujitsu Siemens, Nokia and Sun Microsystems systems (Espiner, 2006). Mitnick hacked into the computer of researcher Tsutomu Shimomura at the San Diego Supercomputer center in 1995; Shimomura, an advanced security expert, tracked down Mitnick in Raleigh, NC, leading to his capture (Jacobus, 2000). There was even a movie made in 2000 called "Takedown," based on the hack of

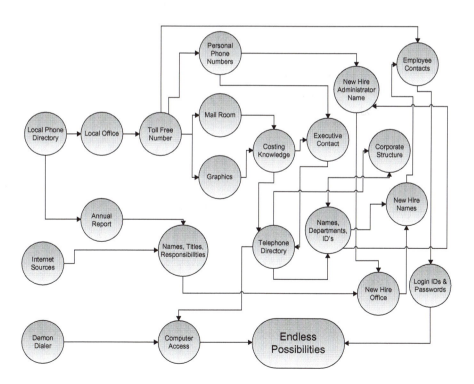

Fig. 2.3. Anatomy of a social engineering attack. Image used with the permission of Winkler (1997).

Shimomura by Mitnick and the ensuing pursuit: http://www.youtube.com/watch?v=L3SKV8kNEhU. He served five years in prison, eight months of which were spent in solitary confinement. After the arrest, he began running a security company that advised organizations and businesses on protecting their places of work from nontechnical attacks. On the topic of new social engineering techniques, Mitnick states social engineers "use the same methods they always have – using a ruse to deceive, influence or trick people into revealing information that benefits the attackers" (Espiner, 2006). Here's a video of Mitnick, telling the story about one of his late-night social engineering escapades with a friend: http://www.youtube.com/watch?v=8L76gTaReeg.

2.2.3 Phishing

Phishing is the attempt to gather private information such as account numbers, passwords, credit card numbers or other personal details by creating a site which looks legitimate. It is possible to create web sites that look identical to a legitimate web site – the only noticeable difference may be in the web address. Even then, it is disguised and not usually noticed by the user. A phisher will send an e-mail which appears to be from a trustworthy organization. The user follows the directions in the e-mail, entering his personal information as requested. Unfortunately, these details are now sent directly to the phisher, and the user has no idea any malicious activity ever occurred ("Benefits," n.d.). This clip shows how simple a phishing attack can be: http://www.youtube.com/watch?v=PRnLSEqzD9c.

Phishing can occur with any web site available. This applies to social media sites as well. Many members list their full names, addresses, birthdays, educational background and current workplace, freely giving out personal information to anyone who wants it. Users have mistakenly entered information and passwords into sites which look similar to their personal accounts but have been faked, giving phishers their social media site information. Againstphishing.com has some simple tips to help keep users safe from phishing. They suggest finding an anti-phishing program that will automatically scan for phishing sites. Furthermore, they recommend users check to make sure the site certificate is valid and the page is secure sockets layer (SSL) secured. Users can also check the web address in the browser address bar to make sure the web site uniform resource locator (URL) is correct. Most importantly, do not click on and follow links from e-mails which seem strange or suspicious ("Phishing," n.d).

2.2.4 Malware

Malware is probably a familiar term for any computer user; security software promises to protect computers from viruses and malware. What exactly is malware? Malware is malicious software that can install on a computer without the user's knowledge or may trick the user into revealing personal information. Malware then propagates and spreads to other users, attempting to reach as many computers as possible. Social media sites are a natural target for malware due to their popularity and large membership.

There are different methods for initial malware attacks: clickjacking, drive-by downloads and password compromise are just a few popular examples. Cybercriminals then attempt to propagate the malware as much as possible by sending direct messages, posting malicious content such as "malvertisements," shortening or obfuscating URL links, installing malicious applications such as a Flash player upgrade, creating fake profiles or sending corrupt e-mails (Orebaugh, 2012).

The Koobface worm is one of the most infamous malware attacks targeting social media and spreads via these networks. It posts a link from an already-infected account to every person to which the infected account is connected. The post usually contains a catchy title, like "Check out this crazy video I found of you!!" Members click on the link and are prompted to upgrade their player, which then installs the Koobface on their computers, repeating the process for each connected member. Although the Koobface is spread through social networking sites, it is installed on users' computers and can access the file system. The Koobface may consist of other types of malware as well, such as spyware, adware, key loggers or Trojan horses ("Koobface," n.d.).

2.2.5 Identity Theft

Identity theft no longer requires a person to steal tangible documentation, such as a driver's license or a bank statement. The Internet and social media have given identity thieves a new and efficient resource for stealing. In the case of social networking, many members describe themselves in their profile, displaying a personal picture and releasing personal information. Only releasing a few pieces of information, such as full name, birth date and address may allow thieves to come up with other basic information not listed on the particular social networking site. Using tools already available on the Internet, such as reverse lookup, they may gather all the information they need to proceed with stealing an identity. From the additional information gathered about a target, it is possible for thieves to forge official documents, such as passports or birth certificates.

Twelve million Americans reported they were victims of identity fraud in 2011 – a 13% increase from the previous year. Furthermore, smartphone owners are one-third more likely to become a casualty of identity fraud than the general public; 62% of these owners do not even password-protect their home screens. In the case of social media sites, LinkedIn has the highest fraud-incident rate at 10%, compared to only 5% for the general population (Waters, 2012). Unfortunately, as more people switch to using smartphones/devices and as social media sites are developed, the amount of identity theft will predicatively increase.

2.2.6 Cyberbullying

The Internet provides a way to share one's thoughts anonymously. It is possible for users to post and comment without having to put their names behind their words. Anonymity, unfortunately, can bring out rude, offensive and malicious behavior in people. Anonymity on the Internet allows users to act and speak in ways which they might not normally have the courage to do in person. Some users do not worry about being anonymous on the Internet; they openly share their hateful thoughts and opinions while proudly displaying their names.

Due to the popularity of social media, and the fact that relationships are the purpose of social networking, it is easy for members to find others they search for. The accessibility of users' profiles provides a new, almost effortless, outlet for those who wish to hassle and harass. Social media has been used to bully, torment and terrorize some members. Cyberbullying has been cited as the cause of extreme distress to some users, leading to violence, self-harm or suicide.

Hoff and Mitchell (2009) define cyberbullying as "'willful and repeated harm inflicted through the medium of electronic text', cyber-bullying puts targets under attack from a barrage of degrading, threatening and/or sexually explicit messages and images conveyed using web sites, instant messaging, blogs, chat rooms, cell phones, web sites, e-mail and personal online profiles." From their research, Hoff and Mitchell

(2009) determined "cyberbullying occurs most commonly from relationship problems; victims experience powerfully negative effects (especially on their social well-being); and the reactive behavior, both from schools and from students, was generally inappropriate or ineffective." They discovered that cyberbullies criticized females most often about their appearance or popularity and taunted males most often about their lack of physical ability or with homophobic remarks.

One of the most recent and highly publicized cyberbullying cases occurred in September 2010 at Rutgers University. Tyler Clementi, an eighteen-year-old freshman, committed suicide by jumping off of the George Washington Bridge after finding out his roommate secretly used a webcam to stream him and another male in their dorm room. Dharun Ravi, Clementi's roommate, had sent messages to friends telling them to connect to his webcam for a "viewing party." Ravi had even posted on Twitter about using a webcam to spy on his roommate having a sexual encounter with another man, which Clementi happened to find. Immediately prior to his death, Clementi made one last post on his Facebook page: "Jumping off the gw bridge sorry." The page has since been turned into a memorial by family, friends and strangers. Ravi went to trial at the Middlesex Superior Court and was charged with fifteen counts, including bias intimidation, invasion of privacy, evidence and witness tampering and hindering apprehension. Ravi was found guilty of all counts on March 16, 2012 ("Tyler," 2012). Ravi was sentenced to 30 days in jail, three years probation, 300 hours of community service, a $10,000 fine and required to attend counseling on cyberbullying and alternate lifestyles (DeMarco, 2012).

According to the 2011 Pew Internet report "Teens, Kindness and Cruelty on Social Network Sites," 88% of teens have witnessed other people being mean or cruel on social network sites. 15% of teens who use social media reported they were the target of cyberbullying. These exchanges occur semiprivately online, since most teens have privacy settings enabled to make sure their profiles are not publically viewable. Among the teens that did experience cruelty or mean behavior on social networking sites, there was no significance relating to age, gender, race, socioeconomic status, or any other demographic measure. Even adults are targets of cyberbullying; 13% reported that someone was mean or cruel to them on social networks. The following word cloud was created by teen participants when describing how they believed people usually acted online (Lenhart et al., 2011) (Fig. 2.4).

Fig. 2.4. Word cloud created from how teens believe users act online. Image used with the permission of Pew Internet & American Life Project.

Here is the most recent review of the State Cyberbullying Laws, compiled by the Cyberbullying Research Center: http://www.cyberbullying.us/Bullying_and_Cyberbullying_Laws.pdf. The review examines state cyberbullying laws and policies (Hinduja and Patchin, 2012), including a brief description for each state.

2.2.7 Cyberstalking

Stalking is a problem that occurs in the corporeal world and one that unfortunately also exists in cyberspace as well. *Police Chief* magazine defines cyberstalking as "an escalated form of online harassment directed at a specific person that causes substantial emotional distress and serves no legitimate purpose. The action is to annoy, alarm and emotionally abuse another person." The *Police Chief* gives examples of cyberstalking such as leaving harassing or threatening messages on a web site, sending inappropriate e-cards, posting personal advertisements in the victim's name, sending viruses, using spyware and hacking into a victim's computer (Hitchcock, 2003).

The Internet provides stalkers with the ability to meet and connect with victims they might never have had an opportunity to find in person. Cyberstalking activities cause anguish to a victim through Internet interactions or electronic environments, such as social media sites, e-mail, chat rooms, bulletin boards, newsgroups, instant messaging and key loggers (Roberts, 2008).

The Mississippi Code of 1972 (as amended) enacted cyberstalking penalties effective in 2003. According to Miss. Code Ann. § 97-45-15 (2003), it is unlawful for a person to:

1. Use in electronic mail or electronic communication any words or language threatening to inflict bodily harm to any person or to that person's child, sibling, spouse or dependent, or physical injury to the property of any person, or for the purpose of extorting money or other things of value from any person.
2. Electronically mail or electronically communicate to another repeatedly, whether or not conversation ensues, for the purpose of threatening, terrifying or harassing any person.
3. Electronically mail or electronically communicate to another and to knowingly make any false statement concerning death, injury, illness, disfigurement, indecent conduct or criminal conduct of the person electronically mailed or of any member of the person's family or household with the intent to threaten, terrify or harass.
4. Knowingly permit an electronic communication device under the person's control to be used for any purpose prohibited by this section.

Cyberstalking is a felony punishable by imprisonment for no more than two years or a fine of no more than five thousand dollars, or both. If the offense violates a restraining order, probation, parole, pretrial release or condition of release or the person has previously been convicted of cyberstalking, it is punishable by imprisonment for no more than five years or a fine of no more than ten thousand dollars or both ("§ 97-45-15," 2003).

A tragic cyberstalking case occurred in New Hampshire in 1999; twenty-year-old Amy Boyer was murdered by her Internet stalker Liam Youens. He perpetrated his cyberstalking through the use of Internet sites and tools available for anyone to use. Through supposed "public information" available online, he found her home address, where she worked, what type of car she drove and other information about Boyer. From the services provided by Internet Service Providers (ISPs), Youens constructed two web sites in Amy Boyer's honor: on one site he listed her personal information and a picture of her, and on the other site he posted his detailed plans on how he was going to murder her. On October 15, 1999, Youens followed through on his plans and murdered Boyer (Tavani and Grodzinksy, 2002).

2.2.8 Cyberthreats/Cyberterrorism

Similar to how social media can be used to threaten a specific person, it is possible for users to threaten acts of violence and terrorism to groups and societies on social media sites as well. Cyberthreats and cyberterrorism involve the use of computers and Internet technology to commit crimes such as theft, information sabotage, copyright infractions, distribution of illegal content, industrial espionage, denial of service attacks, trademark infringements and fraud. The main reason cyberthreats and cyberterrorism are rising is due to the fact these acts take place in a virtual environment and is difficult to trace (Singh and Siddiqui, 2011).

Anonymous, a group of hackers, originally formed to play jokes and cause trouble online; Anonymous is now infamous for hacking major corporate and government web sites. In 2010, the group defended Wikileaks founder Julian Assange by cyberattacking any organizations they deemed antagonistic to Assange. In January 2012, the group hacked the sites of the United States Justice Department in addition to a couple of major entertainment companies and trade groups. The next month, Anonymous accessed and posted a conference call regarding their group between the Federal Bureau of Investigation, Scotland Yard, and other agencies. The group has moved on to hacking other organizations such as the Church of Scientology and the Motion Picture Association of America. Anonymous still communicates via chat rooms and forums, coming up with new and original ideas for attacks ("Anonymous," 2012).

Terrorist groups such as Al-Qaeda, Hamas and Hezbollah use social media sites to attract members and gather information. About 90% of online organized terrorism involves the use of social media. Groups are able to appeal to new potential members without any border restrictions while also gathering military and political intelligence ("Terrorist," 2012). Al-Qaeda has used social media sites such as forums, blogs and file-sharing sites to distribute video and graphic media. These sites have contained instructions for planning and executing specific acts, such as how to build and detonate improvised explosive devices. Anwar al-Awlaki, a member of Al-Qaeda, understood the power of social media; he used these sites for outreach by performing online sermons, some of which supposedly have been the inspiration behind the Fort Hood shooting, the attempted Times Square plot and the underwear bomber (Soufan, 2012).

Stuxnet, a computer worm discovered in July 2010, infected Iran's Bushehr nuclear reactor, sabotaging the crucial centrifuges. Researchers who studied the worm came to the conclusion it was developed by a large and very sophisticated attacker and the intention was to destroy large systems. Stuxnet looks for specific computer settings, and then injects its own code into that system; it makes changes to a specific system code which monitors factories critical operations (McMillan, 2010). Two years after the worm was originally detected, it was determined that the United States and Israel were behind the deployment of Stuxnet. The worm was intended to infect the Natanz uranium facility in Iran, but Stuxnet broke out and affected thousands of systems worldwide. There are no international regulations, standards or treaties restricting the use of cyberweapons (Glenny, 2012).

The US Department of Defense is putting up forty-two million dollars to fund research into monitoring social networks to track the spread of malicious ideas and misinformation, and discover attempts at advocating uprisings. After the Arab revolutions, DARPA, the Defense Advanced Research Projects Agency, believes monitoring social networks will help detect where any future attacks or revolutions might occur (Ball, 2011).

According to the Georgia Tech Information Security Center and the Georgia Tech Research Institute, there are certain cyberthreats users need to be aware of for 2012: search poisoning, mobile web-based attacks and stolen cyber data use for marketing. Search poisoning occurs when a user clicks on a malicious link in the results from a search engine. Since smartphones have become so widely used, attackers may attempt to damage mobile web browsers. Furthermore, botnets are able to capture user information listed on social networks to then sell to businesses and companies for optimum product marketing. Bo Rotoloni, director of the Georgia Tech Research Institute's Cyber Technology and Information Security Laboratory, said on the issue of cyberthreats, "Our adversaries, whether motivated by monetary gain, political/social ideology or otherwise are becoming increasingly sophisticated and better funded. Acting as individuals or groups, these entities know no boundaries, making cyber security a global problem. We can no longer assume our data is safe sitting behind perimeter-protected networks. Attacks penetrate our systems through ubiquitous protocols, mobile devices and social engineering, circumventing the network perimeter. Our best defense on the growing cyber warfront is found in cooperative education and awareness, best-of-breed tools and robust policy developed collaboratively by industry, academia and government" (Georgia, 2011).

Here is The Emerging Cyberthreats Report 2012 presented at the Georgia Tech Cyber Security Summit in 2011 (GTISC and GTRI, 2011), thoroughly explaining threats users should be aware of: http://www.gtisc.gatech.edu/doc/emerging_cyber_threats_report2012.pdf.

2.2.9 Exploitation

Social media sites are common places for members to distribute and share content. Pictures and photographs are posted publically for others to see or privately for a select person or group. In the Journal of Sexual Addiction & Compulsivity, Weiss and Samenow (2010) explain how social media sites can be a dangerous place for those experiencing problematic sexual behaviors. They state that "as anonymous online connection to sexual content and access to willing partners increases – so do the problems." The Internet is a fast place for meeting, sharing, downloading, streaming, etc.; it is easier than ever to access more profiles, more pictures, more messages and more content. Users with sexual addictions or those attempting recovery have to battle the extreme temptation of social media. Unfortunately, many of these people lose their battles and succumb to the power of the Internet and social media.

Most teenagers have cellular phones or mobile devices capable of taking photographs and sending data, allowing them to send pictures to other users. Some teens use this capability to send funny photographs or share a beautiful picture, while others use this technology to send pornographic images of themselves to boyfriends or girlfriends. Again, through the ease of technology, the forwarding and sharing of initially private photographs, or "sexts," can spread like wildfire with devastating results. Sixteen-year-old Jesse Logan sent nude photographs of herself to her boyfriend, thinking they would stay private between them; however, after their break-up, the photographs were forwarded and shared throughout her high school. She was teased and tormented by her peers. She even went on a local news program with her identity concealed to warn other teens about the terrible effects of sexting. Unfortunately, her constant harassment, pain, and suffering were never alleviated; Logan hung herself in her bedroom on July 3, 2008 (Keys, 2009).

Many minors do not realize, though, they are producing and distributing child pornography. Internet security expert Parry Aftab appeared on the Today show in March, 2009, and explained, "If somebody's under the age of 18, it's child pornography, and even the girl that posted the pictures can be charged. Even at the age of 18, because it was sent to somebody under age, it's disseminating pornography to a minor. There are criminal charges that could be made here." Anyone over the age of eighteen who is found to be involved in child pornography or sexting could be prosecuted and placed on the sex offender registry. Even though most social media sites have policies against the use of pornographic photographs on user profiles, a fourteen-year-old girl from New Jersey posted thirty nude photographs of herself to MySpace. Authorities stated she may face up to seventeen years in prison and will probably have to register as a sex offender (Keys, 2009).

Another serious issue exists among social media sites; sexual predators prowl these sites to search for and contact children and under-age teens to use and exploit. Predators manipulate potential victims with the intention of meeting them in person for sexual encounters in a process known as "online grooming." Grooming usually takes place over an extended period of time and involves the predator attempting to make his victim comfortable, relaxed and at ease. Predators tend to have a lot of patience for the time it takes to groom a victim and are oftentimes working with multiple targets. There are general characteristics that can be applied to online sexual predators, but each victim is different and some of the predator's normal methods will be individualized for each child. SafeTeens.com provides a list of tricks and scams to be on the lookout for:

1. "Let's go private." – leaving a public chat or site to create a private environment in which to communicate.
2. "Where's your computer in the house?" – determining if there are adults present around the computer.
3. "Who's your favorite band? Designer? Film? Gear?" – providing information so that a predator can learn more about a victim and personalize offers such as concert tickets, clothes, CDs, etc.
4. "I know someone who can get you a modeling job." – using flattery to attempt and create a connection.
5. "I know a way you can earn money fast." – offering a way to earn money, which has resulted in webcam prostitution business.
6. "You seem sad. Tell me what's bothering you." – being emotionally available for a victim.
7. "What's your phone number?" – attempting to collect personal information.

8. "If you don't do what I ask, I'll tell your parents, share your photos, etc." – intimidating victims into doing what they are told.
9. "You are the love of my life." – showing love and admiration.

Sexual predators will go to any length in order to connect with victims and exploit them. The sexual exploitation and abuse from grooming does not have to take place during face-to-face meetings. Predators can convince or blackmail their victims into taking nude photographs of themselves or performing sexual acts on a webcam, which may potentially be distributed to other pedophiles (Collier, n.d.).

2.2.10 Sexual Assault/Rape/Prostitution

Though not necessarily a direct cause, social media does create another outlet for offenders to perpetrate the crimes of sexual assault and rape. Rapists are able to become friends and socialize with future victims they meet on social sites. Elliott McDermott, a nineteen-year-old male, befriended three young women of ages twelve, thirteen and fourteen on Facebook, where he initially began messaging them. Police called him "every parent's worst nightmare" – he admitted two charges of rape, three sexual assaults and three counts of grooming after convincing each of the girls to meet him (Telegraph, 2012).

Prostitution is another crime possibly arranged through social media. About 83% of prostitutes have Facebook pages, and one out of four prostitutes actually acquired regular clients from Facebook in 2008 (Venkatesh, 2011). Online prostitution employs the same social media tools other businesses do: workers meet potential clients through sites, message, chat and make meeting arrangements. Escorts.com has many of the same features as Facebook: users can create a profile, add pictures, post personal information, message and chat. The site also consists of reviews of service providers and clients by site members. Although online prostitution is still illegal, it takes prostitutes off of the streets and improves safety by allowing service providers to monitor members and possible abusers, along with allowing members to choose their preferred service providers (Palmer, n.d.).

Just as social media tools are versatile, illegal activities and abuse committed using the tools can be versatile as well. Twenty-six-year-old Justin Strom, also known as "J-Dirt," the leader of a gang known as the Underground Gangster Crips, was indicted by a grand jury of running a prostitution ring in Northern Virginia in 2012. He recruited high school girls at school, at the mall or on the Metro and would then use social media sites to draw them into becoming prostitutes for him. He faces a maximum penalty of life in prison (Pope, 2012).

Craigslist, the online classified ad site, was much publicized in recent years due to the crimes committed by the infamous "Craigslist Killer." Twenty-three-year-old Philip Markoff, a medical student in Boston, killed a woman and held another at gun point whom he met through Craigslist in 2009. He answered their ads for massage services and lured the women to upscale hotels in Boston. Markoff was indicted on a first-degree murder charge, armed assault with the intent to rob, two counts of armed kidnapping, armed robbery and two counts of unlawful possession of a firearm (Goodnough, 2009). He later committed suicide in his Boston jail cell while awaiting trial (Finucane, 2010). Craigslist shut down the erotic services section after Markoff's arrest and removed the category entirely a year later. However, prostitution ads have still appeared on the site in other sections; listings for escorts, body rubs and call girls were also found on Facebook and About.com (Kharif, 2012).

2.2.11 Organized Crime

Due to the ability to form private groups and communicate via personal messages, social media is a beneficial tool for organized crime. Terrorist groups and gangs can use the sites to correspond with current members while attempting to recruit new members. Events and attacks can be coordinated citywide, nationwide and even worldwide through the use of social media.

A credit card cloning and fraud gang was found to use Facebook for communication purposes. The Nigerian leader of the gang used the site to interact with contacts across the country while distributing directions to associates. Gang members would stay online on Facebook via their cell phones so they could all see one another; going offline would signal to other members they had been arrested. When the first four members were arrested and their phones seized and switched off, it alerted the other members they had been found out ("Credit," 2012).

In Sao Paulo, Brazil, a kidnapping ring was uncovered in 2010. The kidnappers searched social network profiles to find victims who appeared to be wealthy; the group members then discovered the target's place of employment or favorite bars or clubs. The kidnappers looked for posts regarding expensive trips, nice cars and big houses. After casing a specific profile and determining how much a person would be worth for ransom, they would be able to insist relatives pay to release the kidnapped victims ("Brazil," 2010).

According to Andy Spruill, the Senior Director of Risk Management at Guidance Software, gang members use social media and chats to discuss gang activities, such as the planning and execution of crimes, drug cultivation and distribution and the buying and selling of weapons. These pages promote gang culture and their specific street gangs. Members who will never say a word about their activities when questioned will have folder after folder in their computers fully documenting their gang lifestyle. In August 2009, Jason Aguirre, a known gang member in Orange County, California, was found guilty of first-degree murder for shooting a teen boy and wounding two other family members. Digital evidence was the major evidential factor in giving Aguirre the death penalty (Spruill, 2009). Further information about the Aguirre case can be found here (Spruill and Rackleff, 2009): http://www.lawofficer.com/article/investigation/digital-evidence.

2.3 CONCLUSION

Social media sites are commonly used by members to share personal information, communicate with friends and meet others with similar interests. Consumers, businesses, and organizations have also discovered the benefits of using media sites for advertising and promoting products and causes.

Just as social media sites can be used for a wide variety of valuable and beneficial causes, they can be abused and used for illegal and nefarious activities. Many of the traditional crimes are now perpetrated in the realm of cyberspace. It is important to be aware of and knowledgeable about the possible threats and offenses that can occur on social media sites. To visualize the discussion about crime occurring on social media, here is an infographic briefly explaining twenty unique cases that took place on Facebook (20 Cases solved by using Facebook, n.d.): http://www.criminaljusticedegreesguide.com/features/20-cases-solved-by-facebook.html.

REFERENCES

20 Cases solved by using Facebook. (n.d.). *Criminal Justice Degrees Guide*. Retrieved September 4, 2012, from <http://www.criminaljusticedegreesguide.com/features/20-cases-solved-by-facebook.html>.

§ 97-45-15. Cyberstalking; penalties. (July 1, 2003). *Mississippi Code of 1972*. Retrieved August 31, 2012, from <http://www.mscode.com/free/statutes/97/045/0015.htm>.

Advertisers. (n.d.). *Luminate*. Retrieved August 4, 2012, from <http://www.luminate.com/advertiser/>.

Almasy, S. (September 30, 2009). Social media an inviting target for cybercriminals. *CNN.com*. Retrieved August 8, 2012, from <http://www.cnn.com/2009/TECH/09/28/dcot.socialmedia.privacy/index.html>.

Anonymous (Internet group). (March 8, 2012). *The New York Times*. Retrieved August 31, 2012, from <http://topics.nytimes.com/top/reference/timestopics/organizations/a/anonymous_internet_group/index.html>.

Ball, J. (August 3, 2011). Pentagon to monitor social networking sites for threats. *The Guardian*. Retrieved August 30, 2012, from <http://www.guardian.co.uk/world/2011/aug/03/pentagon-monitor-social-networking-threats>.

Benefits of automatic phishing detection. (n.d.). *Againstphishing*. Retrieved August 9, 2012, from <http://www.againstphishing.com/benefits-phishing-detection.html>.

Brazil police bust kidnappers who browsed social-networking sites for victims. (August 2, 2010). *Fox News*. Retrieved September 4, 2012, from <http://www.foxnews.com/world/2010/08/02/brazil-police-bust-kidnappers-browsed-social-networking-sites-victims/>.

Byford, S. (May 6, 2012). Real-time Facebook "likes" displayed on Brazilian fashion retailer's clothes racks. *The Verge*. Retrieved August 4, 2012, from <http://www.theverge.com/2012/5/6/3002270/fashion-like-facebook-brazil-cea-clothes>.

Clementi, T. (March 16, 2012). *The New York Times*. Retrieved August 29, 2012, from <http://topics.nytimes.com/top/reference/timestopics/people/c/tyler_clementi/index.html>.

Collier, A. (n.d.). How to recognize grooming. *SafeTeens.com*. Retrieved September 3, 2012, from <http://www.safeteens.com/how-to-recognize-grooming/>.

Credit card cloning gang: Fraudsters used social networking site, reveal Ahmedabad Police. (June 14, 2012). *The Times Of India*. Retrieved September 4, 2012, from <http://articles.timesofindia.indiatimes.com/2012-06-14/ahmedabad/32234837_1_nigerian-gang-crime-branch-social-networking>.

DeMarco, M. (May 21, 2012). Dharun Ravi sentenced to 30 days in jail. *NJ.com*. Retrieved September 9, 2012, from <http://www.nj.com/news/index.ssf/2012/05/dharun>.

Espiner, T. (June 14, 2006). Kevin Mitnick, the great pretender. *CNET News*. Retrieved August 8, 2012, from <http://news.cnet.com/kevin-mitnick,-the-great-pretender/2008-1029_3-6083668.html>.

Finucane, M. (August 17, 2010). DA: Markoff fashioned "primitive scalpel" to kill himself. *Boston.com*. Retrieved September 4, 2012, from <http://www.boston.com/news/local/breaking_news/2010/08/da_markoff_fash.html>.

Foursqaure merchant platform. (n.d.). *Foursquare*. Retrieved August 4, 2012, from <https://foursquare.com/business/merchants>.

Georgia Institute of Technology. (October 11, 2011). Cyber threats forecast for 2012 released. *Science Daily*. Retrieved August 30, 2012, from <http://www.sciencedaily.com/releases/2011/10/111011132050.htm>.

Glenny, M. (June 24, 2012). A weapon we can't control. *The New York Times*. Retrieved August 31, 2012, from <http://www.nytimes.com/2012/06/25/opinion/stuxnet-will-come-back-to-haunt-us.html>.

Goodnough, A. (June 21, 2009). Medical student is indicted in Craigslist killing. *The New York Times*. Retrieved September 4, 2012, from <http://www.nytimes.com/2009/06/22/us/22indict. html?_r=2>.

GTISC and GTRI. (2011). Emerging cyber threats report 2012. *Georgia Tech Cyber Security Summit 2011*. Retrieved August 30, 2012, from <www.gtisc.gatech.edu/doc/emerging_cyber_ threats_report2012.pdf>.

Hinduja, S., and Patchin, J. (2012). State cyberbullying laws. *Cyberbullying Research Center*. Retrieved August 29, 2012, from <http://www.cyberbullying.us/Bullying_and_Cyberbullying_ Laws.pdf>.

Hinkley, C. (November 11, 2010). Social media makes way for social engineering. *SecurityWeek. Com*. Retrieved August 8, 2012, from <http://www.securityweek.com/social-media-makes-way-social-engineering>.

Hitchcock, J. (2003). Cyberstalking and law enforcement. *Police Chief Magazine, 70*(12). Retrieved August 12, 2003, from <http://www.policechiefmagazine.org/magazine/index. cfm?fuseaction=display_arch&article_id=166&issue_id=122003>.

Hoff, D., and Mitchell, S. (2009). Cyberbullying: causes, effects, and remedies. *Journal of Educational Administration, 47*(5), 652–665. Retrieved August 24, 2012, from <http://ezproxy.marshall.edu:2116/journals.htm?issn=0957-8234&volume=47&issue=5&articleid=1812293&show= html>.

Jacobus, P. (September 21, 2000). Mitnick released from prison. *CNET News*. Retrieved August 8, 2012, from <http://news.cnet.com/Mitnick-released-from-prison/2100-1023_3-235933.html>.

Jonas, (April 13, 2011). An image is worth a thousand customers – ThingLink and Savalanche join forces to introduce a new image-based social shopping model. *ThingLink Blog*. Retrieved August 4, 2012, from <http://thinglinkblog.com/2011/04/13/an-image-is-worth-a-thousand-customers-thinglink-and-savalanche-join-forces-to-introduce-a-new-image-based-social-shopping-model/>.

Keys, M. (August 14, 2009). Sexting shatters lives, turns children into sex offenders. *KTXL FOX40*. Retrieved September 3, 2012, from <http://www.fox40.com/news/headlines/ktxl-news-sexting0814,0,485577,print.story>.

Kharif, O. (May 24, 2012). Craigslist prostitution ads resurface in some places, study says. *Bloomberg*. Retrieved September 4, 2012, from <http://www.bloomberg.com/news/2012-05-24/ craigslist-prostitution-ads-resurface-in-some-places-study-says.html>.

Koobface – What is it really? (n.d.). *Thats Nonsense!*. Retrieved August 9, 2012, from <http:// www.thatsnonsense.com/viewdef.php?article=koobface_virus>.

Lenhart, A., Madden, M., Smith, A., Purcell, K., Zickuhr, K., and Raine, L. (November 9, 2011). Teens, kindness and cruelty on social network sites. *Pew Internet*. Retrieved August 29, 2012, from <http://pewinternet.org/~/media/Files/Reports/2011/PIP_Teens_Kindness_Cruelty_SNS_Report_ Nov_2011_FINAL_110711.pdf>.

Lovejoy, K., and Saxton, G. (2012). Information, community, and action: How nonprofit organizations use social media. *Journal of Computer-Mediated Communication, 17*(3), 337–353. Retrieved August 5, 2012, from <http://onlinelibrary.wiley.com/doi/10.1111/j.1083-6101.2012.01576.x/pdf>.

McCorvey, J. (January 25, 2010). How to use social networking sites to drive business. *Inc.* Retrieved August 4, 2012, from <http://www.inc.com/guides/using-social-networking-sites.html>.

McMillan, R. (September 21, 2010). Was Stuxnet built to attack Iran's nuclear program? *PCWorld* Retrieved August 31, 2012, from <http://www.pcworld.com/businesscenter/article/205827/was_ stuxnet_built_to_attack_irans_nuclear_program.html>.

Merchant dashboard. (n.d.). *foursquare*. Retrieved August 4, 2012, from <https://foursquare.com/ business/merchants/dashboard>.

Norton cybercrime report 2011. (2011). *Norton*. Retrieved August 8, 2012, from <http://us.norton. com/cybercrimereport/promo>.

Orebaugh, A. (2012). Social media malware. *IAnewsletter*, *15*(2), 4–6. Retrieved August 9, 2012, from <http://iac.dtic.mil/iatac/download/Vol15_No2.pdf>.

Palmer, K. (n.d.). Do escorts use the social media better than corporate America? *Social Media Answers*. Retrieved September 4, 2012, from <www.convertiv.com/do-escorts-use-the-social-media-better-than-corporate-america/>.

Phishing through website duplication. (n.d.). *Againstphishing*. Retrieved August 9, 2012, from <http://www.againstphishing.com/website-duplication.html>.

Pope, M. (April 27, 2012). Prostitution ring recruited women at school, on social media. *WAMU 88.5 – American University Radio*. Retrieved September 4, 2012, from <http://wamu.org/news/morning_edition/12/04/27/prostitution_ring_recruited_women_at_school_on_social_media>.

Roberts, L. (2008). Jurisdictional and definitional concerns with computer-mediated interpersonal crimes: An analysis on cyberstalking. *International Journal of Cyber Criminology*, *2*(1), 271–285. Retrieved August 31, 2012, from <http://www.cybercrimejournal.com/lynnerobertsijccjan2008. pdf>.

Singh, A., and Siddiqui, A. (2011). New face of terror: Cyber threats, e-mails containing viruses. *Asian Journal of Technology & Management Research*, *1*(1), 1–2. Retrieved August 31, 2012, from <http://www.ajtmr.com/papers/vol1issue1/CyberTerror.pdf>.

Smith, A. (2011). 22% of online Americans used social networking or Twitter for politics in 2010 campaign. *Pew Internet*. Retrieved August 5, 2012, from <pewinternet.org/~/media//Files/Reports/2011/PIP-Social-Media-and-2010-Election.pdf>.

Soufan Group, (2012). *TSG Intel brief: Cyber series: Terrorism and social media*. New York, NY: *The Soufan Group*. Retrieved August 30, 2012, from <http://www.soufangroup.com/briefs/details/?Article_Id=272>.

Spruill, A. (2009). Don't fool yourself: Gangs blog and tweet like we do. *DFI News*. Retrieved September 4, 2012, from <http://www.dfinews.com/article/don%E2%80%99t-fool-yourself-gangs-blog-and-tweet-we-do?page=0,0>.

Spruill, A., and Rackleff, T. (2009). Digital evidence. *LawOfficer*. Retrieved September 4, 2012, from <http://www.lawofficer.com/article/investigation/digital-evidence>.

Stutzman, F. (n.d.). An evaluation of identity-sharing behavior in social network communities. *The University of North Carolina at Chapel Hill – School of Information and Library Science*. Retrieved August 4, 2012, from <www.units.muohio.edu/codeconference/papers/papers/stutzman_track5.pdf>.

Tavani, H., and Grodzinsky, F. (2002). Cyberstalking, personal privacy, and moral responsibility. *Ethics and Information Technology*, *4*(2), 123–132. Retrieved August 31, 2012, from <http://ezproxy.marshall.edu:2160/content/klk45j454m882r75/fulltext.pdf>.

Telegraph reporters. (July 2, 2012). Internet predator, 19, who raped girls is "every parent's worst nightmare." *The Telegraph*. Retrieved September 3, 2012, from <www.telegraph.co.uk/technology/facebook/9371220/Internet-predator-19-who-raped-girls-is-every-parents-worst-nightmare. html>.

Terrorist groups recruiting through social media. (January 10, 2012). *CBC News*. Retrieved September 4, 2012, from <http://www.cbc.ca/news/technology/story/2012/01/10/tech-terrorist-social-media.html>.

Thomson, S. (2012). *Political organizations and social media*. Franklin W. Olin College of Engineering. Retrieved August 5, 2012, from <digitalcommons.olin.edu/ahs_capstone_2012/1/>.

Venkatesh, S. (2011). How tech tools transformed New York's sex trade. *Wired*. Retrieved September 4, 2012, from <http://www.wired.com/magazine/2011/01/ff_sextrade/all/1>.

Waters, J. (2012). Why ID thieves love social media. *The Wall Street Journal*. Retrieved August 24, 2012, from <http://online.wsj.com/article/SB10001424052702304636404577293851428596744. html>.

Weiss, R., and Samenow, C. (2010). Smart phones, social networking, sexting and problematic sexual behaviors – A call for research. *Sexual Addiction & Compulsivity, 17*(4), 241–246. Retrieved September 3, 2012, from <http://ezproxy.marshall.edu:2536/ehost/pdfviewer/pdfviewer?sid=103f53b9-0cff-45a5-8b9e-efe871b35e09%40sessionmgr11&vid = 5&hid = 24>.

Winkler, I. (1997). *Corporate espionage: What it is, why it is happening in your company, what you must do about it.* Rocklin, CA: Prima Pub.

CHAPTER 3

Investigative Uses of Social Media

3.1 INTRODUCTION

How Social Media Has Changed the Face of Investigations

As society approaches the so-called "social media revolution," the use of online social media sites has been integrated into everyday affairs. After examining the widespread activity and membership of social sites, it can be concluded that users have merged social media into their daily lives. In effect, social media has become a major part of our functioning society. Crime is a natural consequence of any functioning society; when communities are formed, parts of that functioning society will have criminal aspects. Since social media communities have become a part of daily life, criminal endeavors have naturally been incorporated into people's daily lives as well. It can be understood that social media not only changes how law enforcement investigates criminal activity, but it also changes the professional standards of the organization through its official use capabilities.

3.2 LEVERAGING THE "WAVE" – UTILIZING SOCIAL MEDIA FOR OFFICIAL DEPARTMENT USE

As criminal enterprises have begun to leverage social media as part of its enterprises, law enforcement agencies are quickly adopting such technology as part of their departmental operations and goals as well. Law enforcement agencies use social media for crime investigation, listening/monitoring, intelligence, soliciting tips on crime, notifying the public of crime problems, emergency or disaster-related issues, crime prevention activities, community outreach/citizen engagement, public relations/reputation management, in-service training, recruitment and background investigations of job candidates to name a few ("2011 IACP," 2011, p. 3). In a recent 2011 survey by the International Association of Chiefs of Police (IACP), 88.1% of law enforcement agencies use social media out of the 800 law enforcement agencies surveyed ("2011 IACP," 2011, p. 1). In addition, more than half reported that social media has helped solve crimes and improved police/

community relations within their jurisdiction ("2011 IACP," 2011). Traditionally thought of as merely an investigative tool, social media has provided law enforcement agencies with a nontraditional public voice in the war on crime.

3.2.1 Facebook and Twitter – A Law Enforcement Agency's Most Underrated Resource

If you are not new to Facebook or Twitter, you have probably discovered that many local agencies have developed Facebook and Twitter profiles for the dissemination of various types of information to the general public. According to the IACP study, 75.5% of agencies using social media maintain an active Facebook account ("2011 IACP," 2011, p. 6). Many of these departments provide a one-dimensional approach with these social media accounts, while others use it as a multifaceted tool. Law enforcement may use social media pages like Facebook and Twitter to assist in the community by "promoting better communications, providing greater access to information, fostering greater transparency, allowing for great accountability, encouraging broader participation and providing a vehicle for collaborative problem solving."(Leary and Rappaport, 2008). To assist in this recognized need, Facebook has published a "Best Practices for Police Departments Guide" that can be found at   https://developers.facebook.com/attachment/PagesGuide_Police.pdf. As sites like Facebook and Twitter continue to grow, extending across demographical, age, and even racial barriers, law enforcement agencies will continue to use this capability and more than likely will increasingly use these tools for such purposes in the upcoming future.

3.2.2 Social Media as a Recruitment Tool

It's always been an understated fact that poor recruitment and the limited selection pool of qualified potential law enforcement candidates has been an extreme issue for agencies across the country. In a field that maintains high selection standards due to the job duties and overall trust associated with the job in general, a long list of candidates can dwindle down to a minute number very quickly. Coupled with the harsh reality of the number of agencies continuously looking for qualified officers, such careers can go unadvertised and unnoticed to the potential top candidates for the position. To counter this issue, many agencies have begun to leverage web presence and social media as a means to advertise potential job openings and specifics of the position such as salary, job duties and scheduled test dates to maximize the

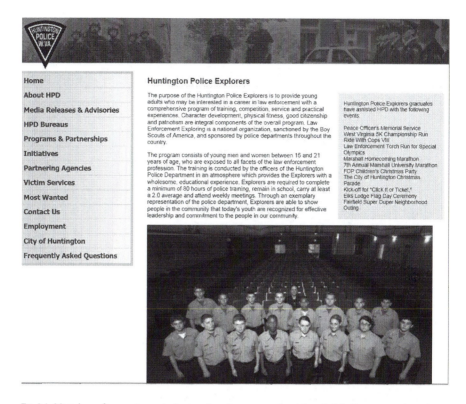

Fig. 3.1. Many law enforcement agencies leverage its web presence and social media following to expand recruitment and applicant interest in their department. (Image courtesy of Huntington Police Department)

number of qualified recruits (Social, 2010). Many agencies also use social media to promote volunteer service programs. For instance, the City of Huntington in West Virginia uses social media and the web as a recruitment tool for its "Explorers" program, a volunteer initiative designed to attract and educate young high school and college individuals who might be interested in a future career in law enforcement (Fig. 3.1).

3.2.3 Social Media as a Community Outreach Tool

Many law enforcement agencies actively maintain various types of community-related initiatives to spurn and maintain community involvement in the efforts to reduce crime. In recent years, many agencies have taken efforts to create a "community policing" model, which is, in essence, collaboration between the police and the community that identifies and solves community problems. Since most members of the

Huntington Police

We would like to encourage everyone to take a look and "Like" the Huntington Neighborhood Watch page. http://www.facebook.com/huntingtonnw

Huntington Neighborhood Watch

"Improving our Community One Step at a Time!"
Page: **75 like this**

Like · Comment · Share · August 2 at 10:59am · 🌐

👍 **46 people like this.**

Write a comment...

Fig. 3.2. Many departments encourage social media followers to engage in community policing initiatives by means of social media. (Image courtesy of Huntington Police Department)

community actively use social media, many agencies are finding that community involvement by means of social media has helped propagate such community policing initiatives (Fig. 3.2).

3.2.4 Utilizing Social Media for Crime Control and Public Information Exchange

Many law enforcement agencies across the United States, from local to state to federal, have leveraged social media as a means for crime control and crime deterrence. Traditionally left as the responsibility of print and television media outlets, social media provides law enforcement with the means to quickly and efficiently disseminate information on crime statistics, crime prevention methods and even agency updates. For instance, the Federal Bureau of Investigation (FBI) actively maintains a Facebook page in addition to their web page (www.facebook.com/FBI) that routinely provides updates on most-wanted offenders, cybercrime updates, etc. City and municipal jurisdictions have also benefitted from an active social media presence as well. The Seattle Police Department distributes information about crimes under investigation via social media, such as pictures and license plates (Hanson, 2011). As of 2012, the department's page has generated over four thousand "likes" and continues to rise in popularity. These updates have also spurred additional social media pages to be created by the city authorities. In 2011, Seattle recently developed a Twitter feed called "Get Your Car Back" – an initiative in which 911 call center staff tweets and updates information about stolen cars (Hanson, 2011). Other smaller jurisdictions, such as the Huntington Police Department in West Virginia, have seen crime statistics at decade lows in the wake of social media involvement and presence (http://www.facebook.com/huntington.police).

Another nontraditional approach to crime control using social media and Internet presence was developed by the Milwaukee Police Department in Milwaukee, Wisconsin. Developing a web page that has the appearance of a Fortune 500 company rather than a governmental entity, the city police department actively maintains a "police news" page that is built quite simply for community awareness and public involvement. The web site, located at www.milwaukeepolicenews.com is used to provide the community with up-to-date information on officers, crime statistics and most-wanted offenders (Vielmetti, 2012). The site offers sections titled "the source," "heroes," "most wanted" and "the stats." The site consists of a user-friendly metro-style interface that allows the user to feel interactive with their browsing experience. In addition, the department also eliminated its traditional weekly press briefings, opting instead to present current investigation info, crime statistics and videos on the site for accuracy and easy access for both journalists and the community. In the end, the city created a social media presence that does not feel or look anything like a traditional governmental web site (Smithsonian, 2012) (Fig. 3.3).

3.2.5 Social Media and Speed of Distribution – A Valuable Commodity for Law Enforcement

Few would argue that social media has provided an unprecedented rise in how information is disseminated to the general public. What sometimes took hours, if not days or months to distribute by means of print or television media, can now be updated in a Facebook status update or simple Twitter posting in a matter of milliseconds. Police have found this extremely useful to inform followers of potential threats or concerns, or provide real-time updates on substantial events, such as the capture of a most-wanted suspect. Samantha Gwinn, Government Solutions Consultant for LexisNexis Risk Solutions, stated in a 2012 article that "Investigation and analysis of social media content provides a huge opportunity in terms of crime prevention and offender

Fig. 3.3. The Milwaukee, Wisconsin, Police Department has taken a nontraditional approach to web-based social media distribution through actively maintaining a highly interactive "police news" page that is built for community awareness and public involvement. (Image courtesy of Milwaukee Police Department)

apprehension" (Role, 2012). This opportunity provides law enforcement with a viable and favorable public outlet to promote better communications, provide greater access to information, foster greater transparency, allow for increased accountability, encourage broader participation and provide a vehicle for collaborative community problem-solving (Leary and Rappaport, 2008) (Fig. 3.4).

3.2.6 Social Media and "Amber Alerts"

In addition to real-time crime updates, social media has also proved to be a valuable tool for updates and investigative leads involving child kidnapping, child exploitation and "Amber Alert" notifications. According to National Center for Missing and Exploited Children (NCMEC), social media has helped to resolve and recover 98.5% of Amber alerts since 2005. Of 1,451 notifications from 2005 to 2009, 1,430 children have been found (National Center for Missing and Exploited Children, 2012). With the amount of Facebook users approaching 901 million as of the end of March 2012, with 20% of this total number in the United States alone (Press@fb.com, n.d.), the likelihood of public intervention and providing of relevant information to

Huntington Police shared a link.

Huntington police arrest murder suspect
www.wowktv.com

The suspect in a July 5 murder in Huntington now is behind bars.

Like · Comment · Share · August 3 at 11:11am ·

👍 32 people like this.

🗂 1 share

Write a comment...

Fig. 3.4. Police have leveraged the speed of social media to provide real-time updates on events of public interest, such as the capture of violent offenders. (Image courtesy of Huntington Police Department)

law enforcement authorities is highly likely and should be considered one of the most powerful tools in the safe return of missing or kidnapped children.

3.2.7 Social Media and Sex Offender Registries

Every state in the United States possesses some kind of mechanism for citizens to actively search for and track previously convicted and currently registered sex offenders based upon geographical location. With the recent advances in social media and web-based technology, users can now delimit searches to include only registered offenders within a particular radius and can obtain a wealth of information about each offender such as conviction type, conviction date, residence address and even a picture. Most states require sex offenders to register and report multiple times a year, and some states have placed tougher restrictions on sex offenders and their use of social media and other publically available Internet resources.

For instance, in June 2012, a new Louisiana law requires sex offenders and child predators to state their criminal status on their Facebook page or other social networking page. This law is the first of its kind in the United States and went effective August 1, 2012. It stands up to constitutional challenges because it expands sex offender registration requirements, common in many states, to include a disclosure on the convicted criminal's social networking sites as well (Martinez, 2012).

On the contrary, however, in the same month, a federal judge upheld an Indiana law banning registered sex offenders from accessing Facebook and other social networking sites used by children, stating that the state has a strong interest in protecting children and that the rest of the Internet remains open to those who have been convicted (Wilson, 2012). Many states have expressed concern over the prevalence and monitoring of convicted predators and their activity on social media sites. Many people argue that social media forums, chat rooms and instant messaging programs effectively create a "virtual playground" for sexual predators to lurk (Wilson, 2012), while others feel that this is a clear violation of first amendment rights for such individuals. As social media propagates, the law and those tasked with monitoring such sexual offenders, such as probation/parole officers, social workers and mental health professionals, will have to be diligent to monitor the social media activity of these individuals within the legal means of the law to ensure that these offenders are not reoffending and relapsing into deviant behavior (Wilson, 2012).

3.2.8 Social Media and Emergency or Disaster-Related Issues

Although considered a use more suited for emergency service personnel than law enforcement, social media has proven to be a valuable resource for the dissemination of emergency and/or disaster-related issues to the population of a given area. Such information could include natural disasters such as hurricanes, tornados, floods and even potential terrorist attacks. In addition, social media can provide citizens with possible evacuation routes, emergency issues such as crimes in progress, and updates on the status of "lockdown" events that may be imposed on public facilities such as schools. Each of these emergency situations have traditionally relied upon law enforcement officers to distribute such information to those affected. With events similar to the 1999 Columbine School Shooting and the "DC Sniper" attacks of 2001 occurring, the quick distribution of relevant information by means of social media could prove to save lives and promote better safety in a time of public panic and confusion ("2011 IACP," 2011, p. 3).

3.2.9 Backlashes of Social Media Use for Law Enforcement

Law enforcement personnel, like many citizens in the general population today, engage in social media activities such as maintaining a personal Facebook page, participating in "blogging" or "tweeting" or otherwise using the Internet for everyday personal use. While much of this activity is perfectly proper and innocuous, in some instances what is said or done by law enforcement personnel on the Internet could be considered detrimental to the department and its mission in a number of ways (IACP, 2011).

With a majority of the US population engaging in the use of social media, it is obvious that law enforcement personnel will use such sites in the same capacity as the general public. Content posted by law enforcement officials on social media sites has the potential to be spread broadly, even if posted under strict privacy settings. Any improper postings can ultimately affect the employee's career and the agency as a whole. Even if content is posted while not performing in an official duty capacity, it can still have detrimental effects to both the professional standards and overall reputation of the agency. Social media site content is now frequently exploited by attorneys in aiming to impugn a law enforcement officer's reputation or show a façade of potential bias. In addition, the safety and security of law enforcement personnel and their families should be of utmost concern. Law enforcement officers and investigators must be made aware of the fact that, regardless of privacy settings, the pictures, the videos and the text (statuses, wall postings, Tweets) they post online could be made available to individuals for whom it was not intended, which could ultimately land in the wrong hands such as a criminal or even so-called "watchdog" groups. It is also important to recognize that social media is becoming increasingly popular and accessible by means of mobile devices such as smartphones and tablet personal computers (PCs). These mobile devices, if owned by the agency, may be subject to a Freedom of Information Act (FOIA) request and could therefore cause significant backlash to both the law enforcement agency and the agent themselves if sensitive information is released (IACP, 2010).

One such case of information being released which was considered detrimental to both a department and law enforcement employee occurred in the case of *Cromer v. Lexington* (2008, U.S. Dist. LEXIS 65374) (E.D. Ky. August 25, 2008) which involved the misconduct of former Lexington Fayette, KY police officer Joshua Cromer following a driving under the influence (DUI) arrest of country music singer John Michael Montgomery. According to court proceedings, the publicity from this arrest due to Montgomery's status as a singer and public figure prompted an increase in the number of visitors to Officer Cromer's

MySpace page. Following the arrest, friends and fellow Lexington PD colleagues posted comments to Cromer's MySpace wall regarding the arrest, including derogatory references to Montgomery and altered photographs depicting Cromer and Montgomery as friends. The MySpace page also revealed inappropriate comments concerning the use of force for his own or his friend's benefit, such as entries regarding a car alarm that was annoying him, not arresting a friend for DUI and inappropriate sexual comments. These postings became the central object of media scrutiny, discrediting Officer Cromer himself as a member of the Division of Police, bringing the Division into ill repute and questioning the operation and efficiency of both the officer and the division. The Lexington City Council issued a decision to terminate Cromer's employment on the grounds of misconduct, inefficiency and insubordination, which was later upheld by both a trial court and Court of Appeals upon a subsequent appeal by Cromer.

Another such case of officer conduct through social media that proved detrimental to a law enforcement agency was in the case of the *City of San Diego v. Roe* (543 U.S. 77) (2004). According to court documents, Roe, who was then an officer of the San Diego Police Department, made a video of himself stripping off his police uniform and masturbating. Roe then sold this video on the Adults-only section of eBay. Roe also sold official police equipment and various other items such as men's underwear on the eBay site. On the site, Roe identified himself as employed in the law enforcement field, but did not divulge his name. Upon discovery by the department, proceedings were initiated that ultimately led to Roe's dismissal from the department. Roe appealed his case to the California Court of Appeals, citing violation of First Amendment rights. The Court ruled in favor of the department, citing that the officer's conduct did not relate to a matter of public concern for First Amendment purposes and, therefore, did not preclude disciplinary action against the officer.

With intense scrutiny placed upon law enforcement agents over sexually explicit communications, communications that could be deemed as derogatory in nature, and social media posts and content in general that could be read by the general public, it is important for agencies to effectively draft protocols that regulate and guide proper social media use among its officers and investigators (IACP, 2010). In addition, agencies should evaluate policies that guide how social media technologies are effectively used for official capacities. Due to the relative newness of social media in the law enforcement public relations community, many of the legal issues surrounding social media have not yet been argued and settled in the court system (IACP, 2010). As legal standards relating to privacy issues are continuously being interpreted at all court levels, the need to ensure that clear standards are in place is more important than ever. Traditionally, agencies have regulated social media usage and postings to that of the designated Public Information Officer (PIO). Additionally, the department/agency should also monitor the presence of "rogue" or "copycat" social media pages that appear to mimic the official department's social media page. The presence of these pages and misleading postings could bring serious backlash and unfavorable public opinion upon the department. If discovered, the agency should promptly notify the legal departments of these social media sites to initiate removal of the copycat pages (see appendix for links to social media law enforcement links and contact information).

3.2.10 Why Isn't Social Media Used More in Investigations? – A Complexity Issue

Although two out of three law enforcement investigators believe that social media helps solve crimes more quickly and effectively (LexisNexis, 2012), why isn't such evidence used more heavily in the course of investigations? In the 2012 study conducted by LexisNexis, 37% of respondents stated that they were unable to access such social media technologies during working hours due to Internet concerns, and 17% did not have the time to use it as a tool. Additionally, 12% stated that the agency policy prohibited such use, while 4% stated that they didn't believe that the information was useful. One of the most alarming statistics was 33% that responded they did not have enough knowledge to use social media as an evidentiary tool (LexisNexis, 2012). Therefore, it's understood that a complexity issue arises in the lack and general availability of effective training to law enforcement investigators tasked with investigating such crimes.

3.2.11 Training and Social Media Investigations

With the lack of affordable and available training to law enforcement investigators, there are issues that arise in how these professionals learn to use social media in the course of their investigations. According to research, 80% of law enforcement professionals are self-taught when it comes to using and leveraging social media for investigations. Many of these investigators become self-trained through personal use and navigating social media sites on their own time (LexisNexis, 2012). A smaller number claim that their investigative knowledge is gleaned from working with colleagues who use social media and gather information. Only 10%, however, claim that their knowledge of social media was obtained through formal training given at the agency (LexisNexis, 2012). As social media continues to grow as a user tool and become more complex, it is ultimately important that the law enforcement community identify and create more opportunities to properly train and keep investigators current on social media investigative methodologies.

There are some opportunities, however, that already exist for law enforcement training in social media investigative methodology. SEARCH, the National Consortium for Justice Information & Statistics, offers an online Investigative Tools & Techniques course for Social Networking sites exclusively for law enforcement investigators (SEARCH – The National Consortium for Justice Information and Statistics, 2012) (http://search.org/programs/hightech/courses/) in addition to other courses that teach the basics of online investigations. Also, the National White Collar Crime Center (NW3C) (2012) based out of Fairmont, West Virginia, offers various training courses exclusively for law enforcement officials, including a Windows Trace Evidence course (http://www.nw3c.org/training/computer-crime/40) which teaches how to recover evidence left behind from Internet activity on a given computer system. Moreover, the NW3C offers basic, intermediate and advanced data recovery and analysis courses for investigators that are tasked with investigating computer crime and collecting evidence from social media networks. Additionally, many federal Internet Crimes against Children (ICAC) task forces offer local training opportunities to members of local agencies, with some of these offerings focused in Internet and social media investigations. It is recommended that investigators become affiliated with local ICAC task forces to not only take advantage of potential training opportunities but affiliate with member agencies (at federal, state and local levels) that may assist in a social media investigation (visit www.icactaskforce.org for more information).

Whether looking for training opportunities or finding a quick answer to a question regarding a social media case or social media technology, joining professional organizations specifically focused on computer and high technology crime is an excellent way for investigators to stay abreast in the field of social media investigations. Organizations such as the International Association of Computer Investigative Specialists (IACIS) (www.iacis.com) and the High Technology Crime Investigation Association (HTCIA) (www.htcia.org) are excellent resources insomuch as they both maintain an active e-mail listserve. E-mail listserves are a great way for investigators to learn about current issues in the digital forensics and technology investigation field. Additionally, members can leverage the expertise and opinion of thousands of qualified members actively engaged in computer-based investigations. This can prove invaluable for those law enforcement investigators tasked with understanding investigating social media crimes (Brown, 2006).

3.3 THE USAGE OF SOCIAL MEDIA IN THE COURSE OF CRIMINAL AND CIVIL INVESTIGATIONS

Social media can provide extremely valuable evidence for investigators. Like any other type of evidence, these sites can provide not only tangible evidence of criminal or civil disobedience – the act itself but can also lend insight into the mind-set of a particular criminal activity – what is commonly referred to in the legal arena as the *mens rea*, or mind-set of the criminal. In criminal cases, law enforcement looks for the presence of the crime itself or corroborating evidence to a crime. On the contrary, a civil investigation pertains more to finding supportive evidence – that is, evidence that supports a claim. Regardless, investigators are collecting the evidence in the same manner. To exemplify, a criminal investigator would collect associates and contacts of a particular gang in the same manner a civil investigator would collect associates and contacts of a particular company or individual associated with such company. With that said, it is imperative that investigators understand not only the intrinsic value of this evidence but how to collect and apply this evidence to a particular investigation. In almost all cases, social media evidence is considered a form of digital evidence, which for intents and puposes, is a relatively new aspect in the field of investigations (Fig. 3.5).

3.3.1 What Is Digital Evidence?

Wherever he steps, whatever he touches, whatever he leaves, even unconsciously, will serve as a silent witness against him. Not only his fingerprints or his footprints, but his hair, the fibers from his clothes, the glass he breaks, the tool mark he leaves, the paint he scratches, the blood or semen he deposits or collects. All of these and more, bear mute witness against him. This is evidence

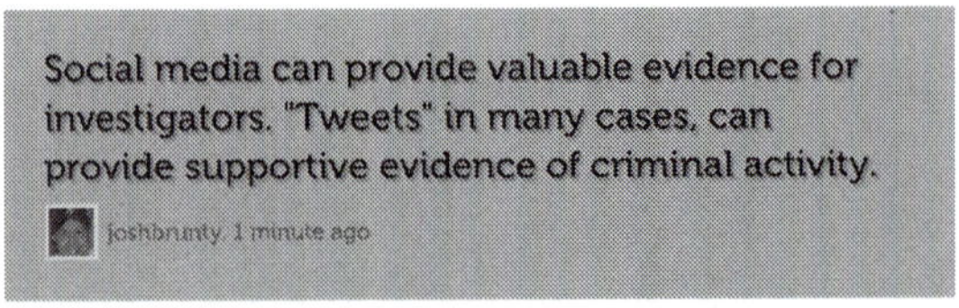

Social media can provide valuable evidence for investigators. "Tweets" in many cases, can provide supportive evidence of criminal activity.

joshbrunty, 1 minute ago

Fig. 3.5. Investigators should examine tweets to determine their relevance in a particular case.

that does not forget. It is not confused by the excitement of the moment. It is not absent because human witnesses are. It is factual evidence. Physical evidence cannot be wrong, it cannot perjure itself, it cannot be wholly absent. Only human failure to find it, study and understand it, can diminish its value.

– Kirk (1953)

To any law enforcement agent or investigator, evidence is crucial to the inquiry and analysis of a particular crime. Evidence, for all intents and purposes, includes everything that is used to determine or demonstrate the truth of an allegation. Collecting and obtaining evidence is the process of using collected items or statements that are either reputed to be true or were themselves proven via evidence, to establish an assertion's truth. In its raw form, social media can be considered a form of evidence, but unlike traditional criminal evidence, social media takes on the unique form of digital evidence. Digital evidence, by definition, is any probative information stored or transmitted in digital form that a party to a court case may use at trial (Casey, 2004). Digital evidence, especially that of social media, tends to be more capacious, more difficult to destroy, easily modified, easily duplicated, potentially more expressive and more readily available than traditional forms of evidence. Much of this evidence can be hidden (or embedded) from the naked eye, can be hard to locate and capture, or can be nearly impossible to obtain without legal intervention such as court orders and search warrants.

In the realm of forensic science, Locard's Exchange Principle is one of the main theories used to explain the exchange of trace evidence within a particular scene of the crime. Trace evidence is any material, such as fibers, fingerprints, and DNA, which has been left or taken from a crime scene. In the field of digital forensics, this principle may still be applied; the evidence left behind exists in cyberspace in digital form.

It is possible for investigators to extract this digital trace evidence, commonly referred to in the digital evidence community as "artifacts" and then perform an analysis. Most users are unaware that they are leaving traces and/or artifacts of their activity behind that is specific to their usage. Knowing where these artifacts are stored can greatly assist in recreating digital events that occurred, such as logging into, chatting, and posting pictures to a particular social media site. Even if a user deletes his Internet history or attempts to remove browsing evidence, artifacts may still be recovered by investigators. Such evidence may be residual on both PC or device and the social media site.

3.3.2 Utilizing Social Media in an Investigative Capacity

Agencies may use social media as an investigative tool when seeking evidence or information about missing or wanted persons, gang participation and web-based crimes such as cyberstalking or cyberbullying (IACP, 2011). For example, prosecutors and attorneys use social network profiles as evidence in cases spanning from underage drinking to child custody. The aforementioned examples are just a few of many instances across the country where police and prosecutors are using information found online and through social networks to put together the pieces of a case and enhance the evidence against an individual (IACP, 2011). According to a recent study performed by LexisNexis in June 2012, four out of five officers used social media for investigative purposes from a total of 1,221 law enforcement professionals surveyed. Of the agencies surveyed, 82% of local and municipal law enforcement agencies utilized social media for investigative purposes, with only 71% of state agencies utilizing social media for the same purposes. Additionally, 86% of cities under 50,000 people utilized social media in some respect, while only 78% of cities over 100,000 people used social media in the same capacity (LexisNexis, 2012).

Social media is considered a valuable tool for law enforcement investigations as investigators in most cases are able to actively see and monitor the activities of a suspect or target in his comfortable setting, while at the same time maintaining a level of anonymity and a virtual "cover" between the investigator and the suspect in question. With the click of a mouse, social media allows law enforcement officers to perform investigative activities that were once hard to obtain (Fig. 3.6).

3.3.3 How Social Media Investigation Is Being Utilized by Law Enforcement

Although the laundry list of social media investigative uses can go on forever and far exceed the confines of this text, the fact that these

updated his profile picture.
September 17,

Fig. 3.6. Law enforcement may use social media as an investigative tool when seeking evidence or information about missing or wanted persons, gang participation, and web-based crimes such as cyberstalking or cyberbullying.

activities are being utilized by employees of law enforcement agencies should be noted and taken into consideration. Although this is not an overly exhaustive list of every way it is being used, the following listings are methods that every law enforcement investigator should utilize in the course of an investigation.

3.3.3.1 Identifying Persons of Interest

With the understanding that a great majority of the American population is using social media in some method or another, it is implied that criminals and suspects in question will more than likely have a social media account such as Facebook, Twitter, MySpace or even YouTube and actively maintain such an account. With that assumption, law enforcement can actively monitor such social media accounts, given that the information is made public and there are no legal constraints in viewing or monitoring such social media presence. In addition to uncovering posts, Tweets, pictures or other probative evidence, law enforcement investigators can also identify associates affiliated with persons of interest (POIs). It is estimated that nearly 80% of investigators utilize this method in the course of their investigation (LexisNexis, 2012). From an intelligence perspective, this can prove to be highly effective in monitoring and breaking up organized crime networks like drug trafficking and prostitution that commonly use social media avenues to promote their criminal activity.

3.3.3.2 Identifying Location of Criminal Activity

With the slow increase in popularity of global positioning systems (GPS) technology and the availability of such technology on mobile devices such as Android and iPhones, social media has leveraged location-based resources that have been integrated into the site itself. This process, known as geolocation, allows users to tag location-based data in a variety of social media applications. In August 2010, Facebook announced the integration of Facebook Places, letting users "check in" to Facebook using a mobile device to let their friends know where they are at the moment (Sharon, 2010). This feature is a derivative of the popular application Foursquare, a social network where users share their geolocation data via mobile phones. Geolocation, in many cases, is commonly overlooked as a means of evidence. Sites such as www.robmenow.com show the seriousness of geolocation data and how criminals can ultimately prey upon unsuspecting citizens who leave their homes unattended. Currently, only half of law enforcement investigators rely upon such evidence, even though it could potentially provide evidence that could incriminate or exonerate a particular individual (LexisNexis, 2012). In 2010, after a series of eighteen burglaries in Nashua, New Hampshire, police suspected that social media and location data was used to facilitate the crimes. After further investigation, Nashua police told MSNBC that most of the burglaries involved homes that were "cased" by the suspects. However, two of the burglaries were directly tied to Facebook posts by the homeowners which indicated that they were away on vacation and had checked in via Facebook "Places." This corroborative evidence was ultimately used to convict the suspects behind the burglary ring (Choney, 2011).

In addition to identifying the location of criminal activity, investigators can use geolocation data to identify and monitor a particular person of interest's whereabouts. This may prove effective in the solving of missing person's cases, fugitives from justice, and even locating kidnapped or missing children (IACP, 2011). Geolocation data may also prove useful to detect patterns in criminal behavior. For instance, as indicated in the above case study, burglars may prey upon absentee homeowners who use geolocated posts to indicate that they are somewhere other than home. Police agencies can use such data to possibly catch such criminals in the act by proactively patrolling such areas of interest, or even identifying patterns or hot spots of particular criminals or criminal networks.

3.3.3.3 Gathering Photographs or Statements to Corroborate Evidence

Often called "fruits of the crime" by those in the legal and criminal justice system, corroborative evidence can sometimes be the make-or-break evidence that determines the validity of a particular criminal case. In the case of social media, both status updates and photographs can sometimes prove the mind-set of a particular criminal and/or assist in retracing the tracks of a suspect to a particular crime. This can be done in many ways and a variety of methods. To exemplify, photographs can place a suspect at a scene in a given period in time. Photographs posted to social media sites can also link suspects to victims or prove the existence of a fact. In addition, postings to social media sites might be corroborated to a particular criminal act. One such example is that of a 2010 Twitter exchange between longtime friends Jameg Blake and Kwame Dancy, both 22, engaging in a verbal crossfire on the microblogging site that wound up with Dancy dead and Blake charged with second-degree murder for killing his longtime friend (Fox News, 2010). Hours before his death, Dancy posted the following message, interpreted by some as directed at Blake:

*n***** is lookin for u don't think I won't give up ya address for a price betta chill asap!*

According to the criminal complaint, a witness saw Blake shoot Dancy in the neck with a shotgun on the street near his home in Manhattan's Harlem section shortly after the heated Twitter exchange. Dancy was subsequently pronounced dead at Harlem Hospital. Blake was arrested two days later and charged with second-degree murder and first-degree manslaughter. In 2011, Blake was sentenced to 21 years in prison primarily due to the corroborative evidence of the angry Twitter exchange (Fractenberg, 2011).

User-uploaded photographs and videos may also prove to be valuable pieces of evidence in a particular investigation. Criminals commonly use social media sites like Facebook and YouTube to upload incriminating photographs and videos of criminal misdeeds. One such case involves that of twenty-three-year-old man videotaping himself driving around in Vancouver, Washington, while brandishing and discharging a pistol out of the window. According to police, the individual then uploaded this footage to YouTube and mentioned it on his Facebook page (Ortiz, 2012). The upload of the video can be found here: http://www.youtube.com/watch?v=kpas4FWJbIs. In many cases, however, videos and pictures can be uploaded to social media outlets with a degree of anonymity. Videos portraying such crimes like arson, burglary, and destruction of property are often uploaded with nonidentifying usernames and/or accounts. It is important to keep in mind that in many cases, the video or image itself may establish probable cause and assist in obtaining a search warrant to request additional information about the uploading account (please read Chapter 4 on how to effectively draft a search warrant statement for social media accounts).

3.3.3.4 Identifying Criminal Activity

Although a broad blanket statement in the sense of the word, law enforcement routinely utilizes social media to identify and convict criminal activity that may show up on sites such as Facebook, Twitter and YouTube. One such example of using social media to identify such activity occurred in Vancouver, British Columbia, in 2011, in which a riot ensued shortly after the Vancouver Canucks lost to the Boston Bruins in the 2011 Stanley Cup Finals. User-uploaded videos (such as this YouTube video showing the start of the riot – http://www.youtube.com/watch?v=XjFM_RswttU&feature=related) began showing up on popular social media websites such as YouTube, Facebook and Twitter at an almost viral pace. At least 140 people were reported as injured during the incident, one critically; at least four people were stabbed, nine police officers were injured, and 101 people were arrested that night, with sixteen further arrests following the event (Bouw, 2011). An investigation team of thirty-plus various municipal agencies was initially set up to investigate individuals of interest who had been seen looting stores, vandalizing buildings and setting fire to cars during the riot (Canadian Broadcasting News, June 16, 2011). More than 1,000,000 photographs and 1,200–1,600 hours of video were recorded by citizens and uploaded to the aforementioned sites (CBC, 2011). In addition, community participation in assisting police to identify the rioters was described as unprecedented with police admitting to being overwhelmed by the amount of evidence of online videos provided (http://www.cbc.ca/news/canada/british-columbia/story/2011/06/20/bc-vancouver-police-riot.html to see how

Fig. 3.7. The overwhelming presence of social media evidence became the primary basis for prosecution (such as the one shown in this destruction of property crime shown above) in the infamous Vancouver Stanley Cup Riots of 2011.

social media played a large part in this overwhelming investigation). As a result of the investigation of such online social media videos, a total of forty people were initially arrested and charged with various crimes such as looting, destruction of property, and burglary to name a few (Mason, 2011) (Fig. 3.7).

3.3.3.5 Cybercasing

Another effective use of social media technologies for law enforcement officials is that of cybercasing. Cybercasing, by definition, has traditionally been reserved as a definition for cybercriminals; it involves using online and location-based data and services to determine when a home is unoccupied with a view to mount real-world attacks (Friedland and Sommer, 2010). As social media sites continue to propagate and archive user-uploaded content on a continuous basis, it is important for law enforcement investigators to realize that a potential wealth of information exists in the casing of such sites. In 2011, Ashland, Kentucky, police officers uncovered an advertisement placed on the popular social media site Craigslist by 59 year-old Otis Adkins soliciting sex from minors while casing the site for potential prostitution. In the advertisement, Adkins offered $300 to meet a fifteen-year-old female respondent, who was actually an undercover Ashland police officer, at a fast food restaurant for sex. Adkins traveled approximately one hour to arrive at the location (WSAZ, 2012). He was in the vehicle he described and arrived at the time he agreed to in an e-mail with undercover task force officers. Investigators say Adkins then approached the undercover officer and talked about obtaining a hotel room and was promptly arrested by West Virginia and Kentucky ICAC officers (http://www.wsaz.com/home/headlines/Branchland_Man_Arrested_in_Ashland_on_Child_Sex_Charge_125555093.html). Scenarios like these aforementioned ones prove that social media sites like Craigslist can be valuable tools in uncovering criminal activity such as prostitution in a given city or area. Many prostitutes use Craigslist to solicit business and easily communicate with potential customers. It is important for law enforcement to recognize the existence of such activity and routinely cybercase such sites for the presence of criminal activity.

3.3.3.6 Identifying POIs
One of the major tasks of any detective or investigator in a given agency is that of identifying POIs in a given investigation. In the days of old, interconnections and relationships between criminals and criminal enterprises were drafted in a notebook or graphing paper, and sometimes took days if not weeks to find relationships between POIs and their relationships with criminal enterprises. Today's social media has changed the face of finding these relationships and has made it quite simple. Investigators can easily identify Facebook acquaintances with the click of a button. In addition, there are various pieces of software, such as Lococitato's Social Media Mapping software. The Facebook, YouTube, Twitter and MySpace Visualizers allow investigators to construct friend and networks based on Facebook user's public profiles and can even detect public links to private profiles (Facebook, Twitter, YouTube Visualizer, 2012). This allows a clickable, animated, visual map to be created which shows the relationships between users of these social media web sites. In networks (especially those criminal enterprises and networks that spread multistate and even multinational), understanding the construction of such criminal networks and connections can prove to be an extremely valuable asset, especially when it comes to deconstructing these enterprises and networks. Not only can federal authorities greatly benefit from such analysis but local municipalities can use this resource to deter crime as well. Therefore, much care must be taken to ensure that this evidence and subsequent analysis is performed legally, effectively and quickly (Figs 3.8 and 3.9).

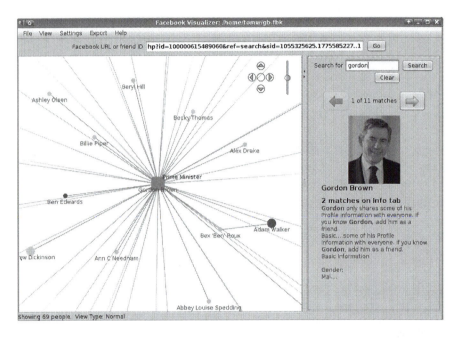

Fig. 3.8. Lococitato's Facebook Visualizer Software allows simplified links to be represented between contacts of a given social media network.

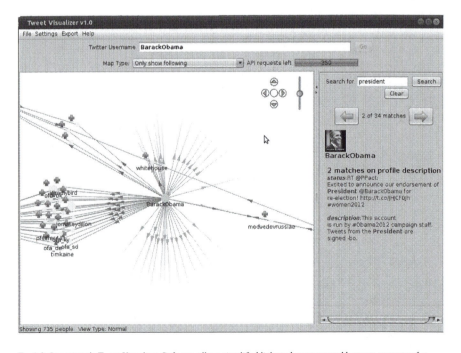

Fig. 3.9. Lococitato's Tweet Visualizer Software allows simplified links to be represented between contacts of a given social media network.

3.4 UNDERSTANDING THE "FORENSICS" OF SOCIAL MEDIA EVIDENCE

3.4.1 Collection and Analysis of Social Media Evidence – How and Where it Is Stored

In order to effectively investigate crimes involving social media, it is imperative that law enforcement understand "how" social media is stored, "where" such information is stored and found and "how" to obtain such information using forensically sound procedures. Social media requires a different mind-set to traditional investigative and current forensic methodologies. This is in addition to the standard, well-established and understood digital forensic processes in which the physical machine (the computer or device) and associated components can be physically seized and reviewed (Lillard, Garrison, Schiller and Steele, 2010). For all intents and purposes, social media evidence is usually found in one of two places: on the machine or device in residual form, and on the network/Internet (stored on the social media site itself). Each of these locations presents individual and unique challenges to the investigator due to the nature of the data and how it must be interpreted. The following section will attempt to explain the location of such data, how to interpret such data, and the challenges of interpreting data left behind and/or stored by social media.

3.4.2 Social Media Artifacts on the Machine or Device

As explained earlier in this section, artifacts of probative evidentiary value can be left behind by users of social media when accessing such sites on PCs and other devices such as mobile phones and tablets. An artifact is a form of trace data (evidence) that is left behind by a particular social media application on a PC or device when an individual accesses such application. Traditionally, social media applications are accessed through an Internet browser (such as Internet Explorer, Firefox, Google Chrome or Safari) and each of these Internet browsers "cache" user data. In some cases, this is also referred to as Temporary Internet Files. Generally, browsers "cache" data to help improve how fast data is opened while browsing the Internet. In most cases, each time a web page is opened, it is sent to your browser's temporary cache on the computer hard drive. If that page is accessed again and has not been modified, the browser will open the page from the previously saved cache instead of downloading the page again. This saves the browser much time insomuch as not having to request the data again and saves the amount of data that needs to be downloaded (Brown, 2006).

A PC that has been legally seized can contain artifacts of social media in these aforementioned cache files. In some cases, the cache may be unreadable and require use of a specialized forensic software tool to access and read these cache files. Software programs such as Magnet Forensics "Internet Evidence Finder – IEF" (Internet Evidence Finder – IEF, 2012) (www.magnetforensics.com) finds existing cache and deleted data from Internet-related communications left behind in the browser cache on a computer hard drive. It then decodes this cached information into a readable form for the investigator to use (Fig. 3.10).

3.4.3 Metadata and Social Media – The Hidden Evidence that Lies Beneath

In addition to cached data by the Internet browser on a seized PC, social media postings may contain metadata, which is simply defined as "data about data." Metadata is merely embedded information that provides additional information about a particular file, web page, video or image (Bargmeyer and Gillman, 1998). In many cases, this metadata is hidden from the user and is mainly used for underlying processing functions. In

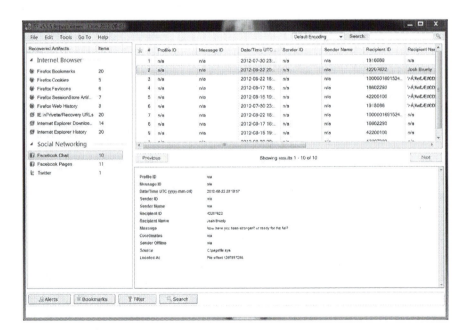

Fig. 3.10. Software like Magnet Forensics Internet Evidence Finder (IEF) has the capability to search and decode artifacts left behind in browser cache space by social media applications. (Image courtesy of Jad Saliba, Magnet Forensics)

the case of Twitter, what normally is only shown as 140 characters to the creator and readers of Twitter posts actually contains a plethora of underlying metadata such as a tweet's unique ID, tweet creation date, the screenname and user ID of the tweet author, and even the timezone and the author's URL (Krickorian, 2012). All of these artifacts can play a huge role to investigators not only in establishing the ID of the author of a particular Twitter "tweet," but also in providing information for search warrant applications to the particular social media service providers.

In addition, Facebook can cache particular metadata pertaining to a particular user or friend's profile. Each Facebook user, upon creation of a Facebook account, is assigned a unique profile ID number, which is normally hidden from the user or only displayed in the address bar. In addition, artifacts such as Facebook chats can retain metadata such as message sent time, message ID (which is assigned to each unique Facebook message) and who it was sent from (Fig. 3.11).

3.4.4 Social Media Artifacts in the "Cloud"
Many of you have heard the term "cloud computing" referred to quite often lately when it comes to storage of digital data. Cloud computing

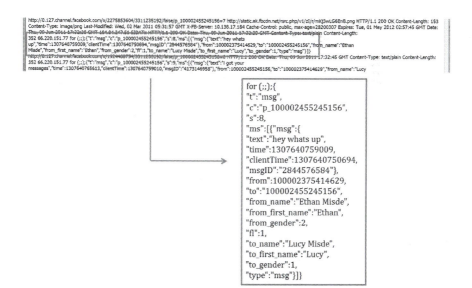

http://0.127.channel.facebook.com/x/2275853604/3311235192/false/p_100002455245196=7 http://static.ak.fbcdn.net/rsrc.php/v1/zI/r/mKJ3wLG6En8.png HTTP/1.1 200 OK Content-Length: 153 Content-Type: image/png Last-Modified: Wed, 02 Mar 2011 05:31:57 GMT X-FB-Server: 10.136.17.184 Cache-Control: public, max-age=28200307 Expires: Tue, 01 May 2012 02:57:45 GMT Date: Thu, 09 Jun 2011 17:32:08 GMT 184.84.247.64 6!DATA HTTP/1.1 200 OK Date: Thu, 09 Jun 2011 17:32:20 GMT Content-Type: text/plain Content-Length: 352 66.220.151.77 for (;;);{"t":"msg","c":"p_100002455245156","s":8,"ms":[{"msg":{"text":"hey whats up","time":1307640759009,"clientTime":1307640750694,"msgID":"2844576584"},"from":100002375414629,"to":"100002455245156","from_name":"Ethan Misde","from_first_name":"Ethan","from_gender":2,"fl":1,"to_name":"Lucy Misde","to_first_name":"Lucy","to_gender":1,"type":"msg"}]}
http://0.127.channel.facebook.com/x/2275853604/3311235192/false/p_100002455245196=9 HTTP/1.1 200 OK Date: Thu, 09 Jun 2011 17:32:45 GMT Content-Type: text/plain Content-Length: 352 66.220.151.77 for (;;);{"t":"msg","c":"p_100002455245156","s":9,"ms":[{"msg":{"text":"I got your messages","time":1307640765613,"clientTime":1307640759010,"msgID":"4173146958"},"from":100002375414629,"to":"100002455245156","from_name":"Lucy

for (;;);{
"t":"msg",
"c":"p_100002455245156",
"s":8,
"ms":[{"msg":{
"text":"hey whats up",
"time":1307640759009,
"clientTime":1307640750694,
"msgID":"2844576584"},
"from":100002375414629,
"to":"100002455245156",
"from_name":"Ethan Misde",
"from_first_name":"Ethan",
"from_gender":2,
"fl":1,
"to_name":"Lucy Misde",
"to_first_name":"Lucy",
"to_gender":1,
"type":"msg"}]}

Fig. 3.11. Metadata, as shown from this capture and breakdown of a single Facebook chat message found in cache data shown above, can yield a plethora of information such as time sent, the user sending it, and even a unique message ID, which Facebook attaches to each unique message.

is use of computing resources that are delivered as a service over a network (typically the Internet) (Lillard et al., 2010). Cloud computing entrusts remote services with a user's data, software and computation, and stores such resources on remote servers that are often owned by the service provider. Social media, for all intents and purposes, is a form of cloud computing; many users use sites like Facebook to archive and store photographs, events, and timelines (Yu, 2012). In order to maintain this interface, sites like Facebook must database this information on their own servers, and make it readily available to users to access (Helenek, Brunty, Fenger & Vance, 2012). It is important for law enforcement investigators to understand that such cloud data is maintained and can be accessed through the proper legal channels. Most social media sites have a dedicated legal team and also maintain guidelines for law enforcement upon asking for information regarding particular users and data related to a particular account. Facebook law enforcement guidelines can be found at http://www.facebook.com/safety/groups/law/guidelines/ while Twitter guidelines can be found at http://support.twitter.com/articles/41949-guidelines-for-law-enforcement#. These sites provide investigators general and specific guidelines and what should be included in legal requests such as preservation orders, court orders, subpoenas and search warrants (please refer to Chapter 4 for more detailed information regarding legal requests and social media). A proper understanding of what to request from social media providers and the proper legal and technical verbiage and information that is to be provided is extremely valuable to law enforcement agents tasked with social media investigations; in many cases this understanding will not only maximize the evidence that is received back from social media service providers but also "weed out" any irrelevant evidence that might be the result of an improper request.

3.4.5 Knowing the Legal Tools of the Trade: The Essential Step to Social Media Investigation

When collecting social media evidence, law enforcement officials must be aware of the legal tools that exist and aid in the acquisition of social media evidence. As explained in further detail in Chapter 4, legal tools such as preservation orders, court orders, subpoenas and search warrants often provide within legally prescribed means the data that might be of relevance to a particular investigation. Although there is much debate and concern over what data law enforcement can legally seize through such documents, social media service providers such as Facebook and Twitter have provided legal assistance and law enforcement liaisons to assist in asking for accurate and legal requests to be processed quickly and efficiently. Although there are hundreds of social media providers out there, there are resources that are publically available to law enforcement investigators in order to obtain contact information for such providers. SEARCH, The National Consortium for Justice Information and Statistics (www.search.org), has compiled and actively maintains a list of Internet Service Providers (ISPs) and the legal contact information for these providers. This information can be found at http://search.org/programs/hightech/isp/ and is invaluable in quickly contacting a particular social media ISP to issue subpoenas, court orders and search warrants.

In addition, social media evidence can be the primary evidence that will allow judges to issue court ordered documents such as search warrants. In order to justify a particular search warrant, law enforcement investigators must establish probable cause. Since social media can sometimes be publically available, this evidence, such as videos or even Facebook pages themselves, can legally be used as the probable cause for a search warrant application. According to the 2012 LexisNexis social media survey, when challenged as evidence, social media evidence provided for search warrants holds up in court 87% of the time (LexisNexis, 2012). As privacy controls and the laws regarding the legal seizure of such data become more stringent, so do the requirements of what can be obtained by a social media driven search warrant (see Chapter 4 for detailed information on search warrants and social media). It is also important for investigators to possess some level of know-how in effectively drafting legal documents that will be accepted by social media service providers such as YouTube, Facebook and Twitter. All too often, the legal counsel of these service providers will reject requests by law enforcement and other authorities because the legal verbiage is incorrect or it does not contain the desired text. This creates an issue with the investigation as the evidence contained on these sites is extremely volatile and subject to change at any time. Therefore, it is important for investigators to become well-versed on the effective drafting of such documents (for more information on drafting effective court orders, see Part 4 and the examples provided in the appendix).

REFERENCES

Bargmeyer, D., and Gillman, D. (1998). Metadata standards and metadata registries: An overview. *Bureau of Labor Statistics.* Retrieved August 27, 2012, from <http://www.bls.gov/ore/pdf/st000010.pdf>.

Bouw, B. (June 20, 2011). Faces in the mob seek forgiveness after Vancouver's Stanley Cup riots. *The Globe and Mail.* Retrieved August 27, 2012<http://www.theglobeandmail.com/news/british-columbia/faces-in-the-mob-seek-forgiveness-after-vancouvers-stanley-cup-riots/article2067208/>.

Brown, C. (2006). Computer evidence: Collection and preservation. Hingham, MA: Thomson/Delmar.

Canadian Broadcasting News, (June 16, 2011). A tale of two riots. *CBC News.* Retrieved July 10, 2012, from <http://www.cbc.ca/news/canada/story/2011/06/16/f-vancouver-riot-1994-2011.html>.

Casey, E. (2004). *Digital evidence and computer crime: Forensic science, computers and the Internet* (2nd ed.). London: Academic Press.

CBC News, (2011, June 20). Police overwhelmed by social media evidence. *CBC News.* Retrieved July 10, 2012, from <http://www.cbc.ca/news/canada/british-columbia/story/2011/06/20/bc-vancouver-police-riot.html>.

City of San Diego v. Roe (543 U.S. 77) (2004).

Choney, S. (2011). Was Facebook and "Places" burglars' roadmap? *NBC News.* Retrieved August 1, 2012, from <http://www.nbcnews.com/technology/technolog/was-facebook-places-burglars-roadmap-127086>.

Cromer v. Lexington (2008 U.S. Dist. LEXIS 65374 (E.D. Ky. August 25, 2008).

Cromer v. Lexington/Fayette Urban County Government (2009). Retrieved August 27, 2012, from <http://www.iacpsocialmedia.org/Resources/CaseLaw/CaseLawDetails.aspx?cmsid=1374&termid=133&depth=2>.

Facebook law enforcement best practices guide. Retrieved September 8, 2012 from <http://www.facebook.com/safety/groups/law/guidelines/>.

Facebook, Twitter, Youtube, Visualizer. Retrieved July 10, 2012 from <www.lococitato.com>.

Fox News, (January 12, 2010). Pals' Twitter messages led to murder, police say. *Fox News.* Retrieved July 10, 2012, from <http://www.foxnews.com/tech/2010/01/12/man-shot-dead-twitter-murder/#ixzz25YF0kxpB>.

Fractenberg, B. (September 21, 2011). Jameg Blake sentenced to 21 years in prison for killing best Friend. *DNAinfo.com.* Retrieved July 10, 2012, from <http://www.dnainfo.com/newyork/20110921/downtown/jameg-blake-sentenced-21-years-prison-for-killing-best-friend#ixzz25YFVqUFL>.

Friedland, G., and Sommer, R. (2010). Cybercasing the joint: On the privacy implications of geotagging. *International Computer Science Institute.* Retrieved August 27, 2012, from <http://www.icsi.berkeley.edu/pubs/networking/cybercasinghotsec10.pdf>.

Hanson, W. (December 2, 2011). How social media is changing law enforcement. *Government Technology: State & Local Government News Articles.* Retrieved August 1, 2012, from <http://www.govtech.com/public-safety/How-Social-Media-Is-Changing-Law-Enforcement.html?page=1>.

Helenek, K., Brunty, J., Fenger, T., and Vance, C. (2012). Do you leave a trace? A forensic analysis of Facebook artifacts. *Proceedings of the 2012 American Academy of Forensic Sciences Conference.* Vol. 18. Baltimore: AAFS.

IACP Center for Social Media. (2011). *2011 IACP Social Media Survey.* Retrieved August 1, 2012, from <www.iacpsocialmedia.org/Portals/1/documents/2011SurveyResults.pdf>.

Internet Evidence Finder – IEF (2012). Retrieved August 27, 2012, from <www.magnetforensics.com>.

Kirk, P. (1953). *Crime Investigation: Physical Evidence and the Police Laboratory*. New York: Interscience Publishers, Inc..

Krickorian, R. (2012). Map of a Twitter status object. *Mehack Blog*. Retrieved August 27, 2012, from <http://mehack.com/map-of-a-twitter-status-object>.

Leary, M. L., and Rappaport, M. (2008). *Beyond the beat: Ethical considerations for community policing in the digital age*. Washington, DC: National Centers for Victims of Crime. Retrieved August 27, 2012, from <www.ncvc.org/ncvc/AGP.Net/Components/documentViewer/Download. aspxnz?DocumentID = 45708>.

Lillard, T., Garrison, C., Schiller, G., and Steele, J. (2010). *Digital forensics for network, Internet, and cloud computing a forensic evidence guide for moving targets and data*. Burlington, MA: Syngress.

Martinez, M. (2012). New La. law: Sex offenders must list status on Facebook, other social media. *CNNTech*. Retrieved July 10, 2012, from <http://articles.cnn.com/2012-06-20/tech/tech_louisiana-sex-offenders-social-media_1_social-networking-offender-registration-facebook-and-myspace? _s=PM:TECH>.

Mason, G. (2011, June 17). The sad, painful truth about the Vancouver rioters' true identities. *Globe and Mail* (Accessed July 10, 2012, from <http://www.theglobeandmail.com/news/national/ british-columbia/gary_mason/the-sad-painful-truth-about-the-vancouver-rioters-true-identities/ article2066321/>.

National Center for Missing and Exploited Children. Retrieved September 3, 2012, from <www. ncmec.org>.

National White Collar Crime Center – NW3C (2012). Windows Internet trace evidence course. Retrieved August 27, 2012, from <http://www.nw3c.org/training/computer-crime/40>.

Ortiz, E. (August 20, 2012). Alleged criminal uploads video of gun-toting drive. *New York Daily News*. Retrieved August 27, 2012, from <http://articles.nydailynews.com/2012-08-20/ news/33290661_1_airsoft-gun-uploads-youtube>.

Press@fb.com. (n.d). Key facts. *Facebook Newsroom*. Retrieved June 19, 2012, from <http://news-room.fb.com/content/default.aspx?NewsAreaId = 22>.

Role of social media in law enforcement significant and growing. (July 18, 2012). *LexisNexis*. Retrieved August 2, 2012, from <http://www.lexisnexis.com/risk/newsevents/press-release.aspx? id=1342623085481181>.

SEARCH – The National Consortium for Justice Information and Statistics (2012). Training courses overview. Retrieved August 27, 2012 from <http://search.org/programs/hightech/courses/>.

Sharon, M. (2010). "Who, what, when, and now…where". *Facebook*. Retrieved August 27, 2012, from <http://blog.facebook.com/blog.php?post=418175202130>.

Smithsonian Magazine (2012). Check out the Milwaukee Police's mind-blowing, crime busting site. *Smithsonian Magazine*. Retrieved August 27, 2012, from <http://blogs.smithsonianmag.com/ smartnews/2012/08/check-out-the-milwaukee-polices-mind-blowing-crime-busting-site/>.

Social media – Concepts and issues paper. (September 2010). *IACP National Law Enforcement Policy Center*. Retrieved August 1, 2012, from <www.iacpsocialmedia.org/Portals/1/documents/ Social%20Media%20Paper.pdf>.

Twitter Guidelines for Law Enforcement. Retrieved September 8, 2012, from <http://sup-port.twitter.com/groups/33-report-abuse-or-policy-violations/topics/148-policy-information/ articles/41949-guidelines-for-law-enforcement#>.

Vielmetti, B. (2012). Milwaukee police website gets nod in advertising age. *Milwaukee Journal Sentinel*. Retrieved August 27, 2012, from <http://www.jsonline.com/blogs/news/167558685.html>.

WSAZ News, (March 6, 2012). Branchland man sentenced on federal child sex charge. *WSAZ News*. Retrieved August 27, 2012, from <http://www.wsaz.com/home/headlines/Branchland_Man_ Arrested_in_Ashland_on_Child_Sex_Charge_125555093.html>.

Wilson, C. (June 25, 2012). Federal judge bans sex offenders from social networking. *The Washington Post*. Retrieved July 10, 2012, from <http://www.washingtonpost.com/politics/federal-judge-bans-sex-offenders-from-social-networking/2012/06/24/gJQAkGRa1V_story.html>.

Yu, R. (March 19, 2012). Social media role in police cases growing. *USATODAY.com*. Retrieved August 2, 2012, from <http://www.usatoday.com/tech/news/story/2012-03-18/social-media-law-enforcement/53614910/1>.

CHAPTER 4

Social Media and the Law: Legal Considerations

4.1 INTRODUCTION

The drive toward a society dependent upon the usage of social media is well upon us. The myriad of social media sites has made it appealing not only as a communication mechanism but also as a method of electronic commerce, information sharing and even advertising. This interlacing of resources being utilized by social media has made them just as useful as the traditional Internet resources (such as chat clients and information searching) Therefore, social media sites are no less vulnerable to unlawful or wrongful activity than more traditional Internet resources; unauthorized access, modification, data leaks, corruption, destruction and all manner of criminal activity are conducted in these unstructured places (Lillard, Garrison, Schiller, & Steele 2010). With the overall community of users using social media increasing exponentially, the reality that criminals will utilize and form part of the social media community will be a difficult obstacle to overcome by investigators of these types of crimes. As is the case in traditional digital forensics and investigations, social media can be the *de facto* evidence for a particular crime or can be corroborating evidence that suggests a particular crime has occurred. As is the case with any types of evidence, there are legal standards and baselines that must be considered and followed when dealing with such data. This section will look at the challenges posed for the collection, preservation and presentation of social media evidence. It is important to note, however, that although there is ample case law and legal baselines that can be applied and interpreted to social media evidence, the relative newness of social media evidence being presented in court leaves very little case law directly pertaining to social media evidence and forensic analysis. This section draws from experienced investigators and practitioners in the field and the case law that is currently guiding social media analysis. This section also looks at the legal constraints that may be faced in the future of social media investigations.

4.2 SOCIAL MEDIA AND THE FIRST AMENDMENT – A CHANGING LANDSCAPE

Across the globe, social media has been at the forefront of communication during natural disasters, revolts against tyranny and civil protests; few methods of speech see more activity than social media sites, in particular Twitter and Facebook. We have already seen governments in Egypt and China infringe online speech from these sites and American courts have recently weighed-in on issues of speech and social media. Simply put, social media and first amendment rights will be challenged in the courts for years if not decades before we are able to gain a clear understanding of the legal underpinning regarding first amendment social media rights. In the law enforcement arena, there is much to be discussed; issues such as what is considered protected or criminal speech and what constitutional rights does a particular possess before it crosses into the realm of criminal behavior are all questions that are in need of clarification and understanding within the investigative community.

Written as is, the first amendment of the US Constitution states:

Congress shall make no law respecting an establishment of religion, or prohibiting the free exercise thereof; or abridging the freedom of speech, or of the press; or the right of the people peaceably to assemble, and to petition the Government for a redress of grievances.

U.S. Const. amend. I

When originally drafted, the First Amendment was only applicable to laws enacted by Congress. However, in *Gitlow v. New York* (268 U.S. 652 (1925)), the Supreme Court applied provisions of the First Amendment to each state, extending the reach of certain limitations on federal government authority set forth in the First Amendment; specifically the provisions protecting freedom of speech and freedom of the press (1925). In addition, both the Supreme Court and lower courts have defined and recognized a series of exceptions and provisions protecting the freedom of speech of certain actions, with many of these exceptions being applied or interpreted by the courts to the issue of social media.

4.2.1 Press "Like" to Continue – Protected Speech and Social Media

One first amendment issue that is at the forefront of court and social media scrutiny is certainly that of freedom of speech. More than ever, social media has made free speech easy and instantaneous, creating legal issues that must be addressed by the courts. Facebook group pages advocating a particular cause can be easily constructed in minutes, and Twitter postings can incite a revolution. With that said, courts are placing social media content under the proverbial microscope to examine first amendment free speech issues. One of the more highly contested aspects of first amendment free speech rights is that of Facebook content and what should be protected. In August 2012, Attorneys for Facebook and the American Civil Liberties Union filed appellate briefs within the fourth circuit US Court of Appeals contesting that clicking the "Like" button on the social networking site is considered constitutionally protected speech under provisions of the first amendment. The case stems from six employees of the Hampton County Sheriff's office in Hampton, VA who were fired by Hampton Sheriff Roberts after they supported his opponent in his 2009 reelection bid, which he won. One of the workers "liked" the Facebook page of Roberts' opponent. The workers sued, saying their First Amendment rights were violated. In the issued opinion ruling, US District Judge Raymond Jackson stated that merely clicking the "Like" button is not sufficient speech to enact first amendment protections (Vergakis, 2012). In the filed amicus brief with the appellate court, Facebook stated that the "Like" button was "the 21st-century equivalent of a front-yard campaign sign." In addition, the brief stated that "liking a Facebook Page is entitled to full First Amendment protection. The district court reached a contrary conclusion based on an apparent misunderstanding of the way Facebook works." (O'Connor, 2012).

4.2.2 First Amendment Exceptions – Application to Social Media

Although the first amendment exists to guarantee free speech and expression, there are exceptions that have been created over time, based on certain types of speech and expression, and under different contexts. Speech that involves incitement, false statements of fact, obscenity (including child pornography), threats, speech owned by others, and speech which diminishes the capacity of the government, are all completely exempt from First Amendment protections. Each of these exemptions carries value when applied to issues within social media.

4.2.3 Incitement and the Clear and Present Danger Test – What It means to Social Media

Originally, speech that presents a danger was established in *Schenck v. the United States* (249 U.S. 47 (1919)) which focused on the constitutionality for printing nearly 15,000 leaflets that advocated opposition to the draft during World War I. These leaflets contained words such as "do not submit to intimidation" and "assert your rights" and other statements that opposed the US government and its involvement and stance on the war. Schenck was indicted and convicted on the grounds of violating the Espionage Act of 1917. Schenck appealed his case to the US Supreme Court, which issued a unanimous opinion that Schenck's criminal conviction was constitutional on the grounds that the first amendment did not protect insubordinate speech, insomuch as the circumstances of wartime permit greater restrictions on free speech than would be tolerated and allowed during periods of peacetime.

In issuing his opinion to the court, Justice Oliver Wendell Holmes stated:

> The most stringent protection of free speech would not protect a man in falsely shouting fire in a theater and causing a panic. The question in every case is whether the words used are used in such circumstances and are of such a nature as to create a clear and present danger that they will bring about the substantive evils that Congress has a right to prevent.
>
> **Schenck vs. U.S. (1917)**

This statement led to the creation of the "clear and present danger" test, which was used as the measuring stick of first amendment speech prosecutions until replaced by the "imminent lawless action" test established in *Brandenburg v. Ohio* (395 U.S. 444 (1969)). In Brandenburg, the US Supreme Court held that the government cannot criminally prosecute speech that is considered inflammatory unless that speech is indicative or is likely to cause "imminent lawless action." This case hinged on the actions of Clarence Brandenburg, a Ku Klux Klan leader in Ohio who contacted and invited a reporter at a Cincinnati television station to cover and film an upcoming KKK rally near Cincinnati in the summer of 1964. Much of the rally was filmed, which revealed several men in robes and hoods, carrying illegal firearms, burning crosses and frequently citing death threats to "niggers" and "Jews." In addition, many of the speeches indicated that the President, Congress and Supreme Court suppressed the white/Caucasian race and advocated violence in an upcoming march upon Washington, DC that was to take place later that summer. Brandenburg was prosecuted for his acts in Ohio state court and subsequently appealed to the US Supreme Court. In issuing its opinion, the Court reversed Brandenburg's conviction, holding that government cannot constitutionally punish the mere advocacy of the usage of force or violation of the law. In his concurring opinion, Justice

William O. Douglas pointed out the appropriate role of symbolic speech in First Amendment doctrine, using examples such as a person ripping up a Bible to celebrate the abandonment of his faith, or tearing a copy of the Constitution in order to protest a Supreme Court decision, or burning a draft card as a means of opposition to war. According to Justice Douglas, all of these aforementioned situations portrayed an action that was a vital way of conveying a certain message, and thus the action itself deserved First Amendment protection (Kissing, 2001). Brandenburg was the last major case that has been argued in regards to inciting speech and lawless action. As of 2012, the Brandenburg test is still the baseline standard used by lower courts to punish incitement or inflammatory speech. Although largely unchallenged since 1969, it can be implied that our ever-changing social media and social networking landscape may revisit this measuring test of free speech.

Social media has created quite the buzz in recent years as it has pushed the envelope of what is considered Speech that presents a "clear and present danger" to the safety of society. Pages such as "kill Barack Obama" have appeared on Facebook, generating both fans and likes (Fig. 4.1). In addition, the Justice Holmes statement of "shouting fire

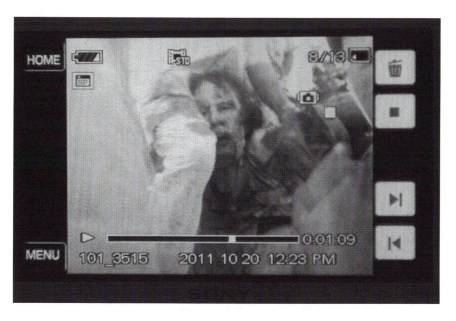

Fig. 4.1. The governmental overthrow in Libya and the eventual capture and death of former Libyan leader Moammer Gadhafi was shared with the world through amateur cell phone videos that were subsequently uploaded to sites such as YouTube and Twitter. Source: Unknown.

in a crowded theater" that became so popular in the *Schenck* case took on a completely new meaning in the form of Twitter postings in July 2012 when an anonymous would-be shooter identified as Anonymous Celebrity and @obamasmistress tweeted "I might just shoot up this theater in New York I know they leave their exit doors locked. Ha now I gotta plan it step." Written from late July to early August 2012, the user describes planning a murder at the theater and tweeted promises of violence to other Twitter users that the threats were genuine and would be followed up (Li, 2012). Although the New York Twitter shooter case presented no Supreme Court free speech challenge, it does show that the prevalence and widespread dissemination of online postings may be an issue that will undoubtedly face the courts in years to come (Ruderman, 2012).

In addition, social media has been the recent driving force behind much of the governmental overthrows and changes in middle–eastern government regimes. In part by using the social networking sites, activists organized and publicized unprecedented protests that gave rise to the so-called "Arab Spring," which as of 2012 has seen longtime governmental regimes in Egypt, Libya and Tunisia fall, regimes in Syria, Yemen and Bahrain clash with the oppositional factions, and leaders in Jordan, Saudi Arabia and the UAE to offer more benefits to their populace (Huang, 2011). Just how important the role that social media had in these revolts and overthrows is debatable, but it is inferred that the sites played a major role in such activity and the spreading of speech to incite an overthrow. In a report released by the Dubai School of Government in 2011 entitled the "Arab Social Media Report," the most popular Twitter hashtags in the Arab region in the first three months of the year were "Egypt," "Jan25," "Libya," "Bahrain" and "protest" (2011). Additionally, according to the report, Facebook usage swelled in these Arab regions between January and April, and in some cases more than doubled. On Twitter, the hashtag "Egypt" had 1.4 million mentions in the three months of the year. The terms "Libya" had 990,000; "Bahrain" had 640,000; and the word "protest" had 620,000. The amount of tweets was shown to have ascended during the turning points of each of these uprisings. The government's efforts to block out such information, the report stated, ended up compelling the populace to be more active and find ways to be more creative about communicating and organizing protests (2011). Social media, its rise, and its new activist uses played a critical role in the mobilization and empowerment, shaping opinions and influencing change. Although not directly a first amendment issue in the United States, one looking in through the window could imply that the magnitude of social media could repave the legal pathway of our first amendment free speech legal landscape in the upcoming years.

4.3 SEARCH AND SEIZURE OF SOCIAL MEDIA – A LEGAL PERSPECTIVE

The fourth amendment of the US Constitution reads as follows:

> *The right of the people to be secure in their persons, houses, papers and effects, against unreasonable searches and seizures, shall not be violated, and no Warrants shall issue, but upon probable cause, supported by Oath or affirmation, and particularly describing the place to be searched, and the persons or things to be seized.*
>
> **U.S. Const. amend. IV**

Although this provision was written in order to protect against physical searches against a person and their property, much of this provision directly applies to that of electronic communication and social media. Over the last decade, courts adjudicated whether the government can access evidence of illegal activity stored on digital medium such as social media without violating the Fourth Amendment. The argument that has caused great consideration is that whether social media users maintain a reasonable expectation of privacy in their online social networking activity such that police investigation is subject to the Fourth Amendment's warrant requirement (Petrashek, 2010).

Interpreted literally, the fourth amendment does not prohibit search and seizure of online communication, but rather holds that that the search and seizure is legal given it is reasonable and adheres to the legal baselines set forth by the courts. Customarily, a search and seizure was held to be legal if the law enforcement agent or agency obtained a warrant for such a search. However, in the world of social media, much of the content is publically available and within plain view, which complicates legal search criteria and creates a "gray area" in regards to which content can be legally seized with and without a search warrant.

4.4 UTILIZING CRIMINAL PROCEDURE TO OBTAIN SOCIAL MEDIA EVIDENCE

4.4.1 Requesting Information from Social Media Sites

In many cases, social media sites such as Twitter and Facebook will only respond in compliance with US law to valid legal process. For example, requests for contents of communication require a US search warrant. Nonpublic information about social users is not released except as lawfully required by appropriate legal process such as a subpoena, court order, search warrant or other valid legal process (which are described in further detail below). Most social media sites disclose account records in accordance with provisions of the federal Stored Communications Act (SCA), 18 USC § 2701–2712.

When investigating criminal activity or evidence contained within social media sites, it is important for investigators to recognize that there are legal tools that exist which can be leveraged to obtain evidence in such investigations. Most social media sites disclose account records in accordance with provisions of the federal Stored Communications Act (SCA), 18 USC § 2701–2712. Generally, under provisions of the SCA, there are four tools that can be used for such evidence: (i) preservation/hold letters, (ii) subpoenas, (iii) court orders and (iv) search warrants.

4.4.1.1 Preservation/Hold Letters

18 U.S.C. § 2703(f)(1) states: "A provider of wire or electronic communication service or a remote computing service, upon the request of a governmental entity, shall take all necessary steps to preserve records and other evidence in its possession pending the issuance of a court order or other process."

Preservation letters, commonly referred to by law enforcement investigators and courts as 2703(f) orders due to its statutory requirements, require social media providers to preserve records that exist at the time the letter is received, but cannot require preservation of future information (such preservation would be considered a form of wiretapping and a violation of Title XXX wiretap restrictions). On receipt of the preservation letter, the social media provider must retain records for a period of up to 90 days. Additional requests may extend this legally specified period in increments of 90 days. Preservation orders can be of extreme value in investigations involving social media as usually such content is volatile, easily changed and subject to change quite frequently, such as a particular Facebook or Twitter user's page. It is important to note, however, that such requests only preserve the data and no additional information such as user information or content provided by the social media provider to the investigator. It is highly recommended that the drafting of a preservation letter should be the first task performed by investigators in a social media investigation to ensure timely notice to the social media providers that an investigation has been initiated and that more information might be requested. For the sake of simplicity, we have provided a Preservation Order template (see Appendix A) that outlines the basic requirements of a 2703(f) order. Although the type of information requesting to be preserved will be different between different social media sites, the template provides a good legally acceptable baseline.

4.4.1.2 Subpoenas

In most cases, criminal agencies can utilize administrative or grand jury subpoenas to obtain digital information from social media service providers. This varies, however, by jurisdiction and the content required by subpoenas can vary between jurisdictions. It is important for investigators to consult prosecutors and/or district attorneys/district courts within a particular jurisdiction to determine whether or not a subpoena can be legally submitted by the court. In many cases, however, subpoenas can yield information from social media providers such as: name, length of service, credit card information, e-mail address(es) and a recent login IP address, if available. These subpoenas are limited by privacy rights set forth in the Electronic Communication Privacy Act (18 USC 2510).

4.4.1.3 Court Orders

Court orders, commonly referred to in the investigative community as "d" orders or 2703(d) orders, are designated such a name due to the provisions set forth for court orders in the US Code 18 USC 2703(d). Court orders usually provide law enforcement disclosure of certain records or other information pertaining to the social media account, not including contents of communications, which may include message headers and IP addresses, in addition to the basic subscriber records that may be provided in a subpoena. Although court orders can provide much evidence in relation to social media investigations, they are not widely used as an investigator must be able to state with "specific and articulable" fact that there is reasonable belief that the targeted information is pertinent to the case. In the case of social media, this may be hard to prove at times due to the mere fact that a given social media site may or may not have relevant corroborating evidence of a particular crime, such as kidnapping, murder or illegal drug activity. Court orders, however, are still helpful to social media investigations as they allow investigators to obtain more than just subscriber information; they are beginning to be leveraged more often by law enforcement to provide transactional information that can prove to be very effective in tracking down and determining use on a specific social media site. It is also worthy to note that social media sites may provide notification to the suspect/user upon issuance of a court order to a law enforcement agency. In some cases, such notification may jeopardize an investigation or lead to risk of harm. In each of these cases, law enforcement can include and establish in the court order that notification or notice to the end-user is prohibited.

4.4.1.4 Search Warrants

Traditionally, search warrants provide investigators with the authority to enter a premises, search for the objects specified in the warrant, and seize such items. Search warrants must be supported by probable cause and the articles of the search must be described with sufficient diligence (Maras, 2011). In most cases, probable cause *exists where the known facts and circumstances are sufficient to warrant a man of reasonable prudence in the belief that contraband or evidence of a crime can be found (Ornellas v. US)*. In the world of social media, however, there are no physical premises or objects; there is only a virtual community to enter such "contraband" or "evidence." Therefore, unlike traditional search warrants, warrants for social media sites must be drafted in such a manner that will be legally acceptable and will provide relevant information back to the investigating officer. Search warrants for social media sites may include messages, photos, videos, wall posts and location information to name a few.

4.4.2 International Legal Process and Social Media – Requests from Non-US Law Enforcement

US law authorizes social media sites to respond to requests for user information from foreign law enforcement agencies that are issued via US court either by way of a mutual legal assistance treaty or a letter rogatory. It is the policy of many social media sites like Facebook and Twitter to comply to such US court-ordered requests.

4.4.3 Emergency Requests from Law Enforcement

There are times in law enforcement investigations, where traditional legal requests must be "bypassed" in a sense and the quick request and provision of social media account information may be of an emergency situation. Matters such as: imminent harm to a child or risk of death or serious physical injury to any person, often cases require information without delay. Most social media sites will only respond and provide emergency information to law enforcement agents. Obtaining this information, in many cases, in child exploitation and child pornography cases, where harm to a child can be proven.

4.4.4 Requesting Social Media Data Under User Consent

A law enforcement investigator can legally request data from social media providers under consent of the user. If an investigator is seeking information about a social media user who has provided consent for the investigator to access or obtain the user's account information, the user should be directed by the investigator to obtain that information on their own from their account. Some sites, such as Facebook, allow users to download all content of their profile into a zip file. In addition, the user can also view recent IP addresses in their Account Settings under Security Settings/Active Sessions. However, users do not have access to historical IP information without going through the aforementioned legal processes.

4.4.5 The Electronic Communications Privacy Act and Social Media Evidence

The legal building blocks regarding the drafting of the aforementioned legal documents used in seizing social media content are primarily based upon the Electronic Communications Privacy Act (ECPA) of 1986. The stored communications chapter of the ECPA was intended to provide customers and subscribers of certain communications service providers with privacy protections. ECPA provides a higher level of privacy protection to the contents of communications and files stored with a provider than to records detailing the use of the service or the subscriber's identity.

ECPA may dictate what type of legal process is necessary to compel a provider to disclose specific types of customer/subscriber information to law enforcement investigators. ECPA also limits what a provider may and may not voluntarily disclose to others, including law enforcement.

ECPA applies when a law enforcement agent seeks certain information from a provider of electronic communications service or remote computing service. Traditionally, this information is usually divided into three major forms: subscriber information, transactional information and the content itself.

4.4.5.1 Basic Subscriber Information

Law enforcement agents may use a search warrant or subpoena, if allowed specifically by their state law, to obtain certain information listed in ECPA relating to the identity of a particular customer/subscriber, the customer/subscriber's relationship with the service provider and basic session connection records. Basic subscriber information also includes such information as: e-mail addresses registered to a particular social media account, user identification numbers (such as those utilized by Twitter and Facebook), date and timestamps of account creation dates, most recent logins and registered mobile phone numbers.

Extensive transactional related records, such as logging information revealing the user information of persons with whom a customer corresponded during prior sessions, are not available by subpoena. However, the use of a search warrant with notice can allow the discovery of the same evidence as a 2703(d) court order and should be utilized when seeking this type of information.

4.4.5.2 Transactional Information

A law enforcement investigator will need to obtain a court order under 18 USC § 2703(d) to compel a provider to disclose more detailed, non-content subscriber and session information, commonly referred to as transactional information, about the use of the services by a customer/subscriber. These records could include account activity logs that reflect what IP addresses the subscriber visited over time and e-mail addresses of others from whom or to whom the subscriber exchanged messages.

Any Federal magistrate or district court with jurisdiction over specific offenses under investigation may issue a 2703(d) court order. As previously stated, the application must offer "specific and articulable facts showing that there are reasonable grounds to believe that... the records or other information sought are relevant and material to an ongoing criminal investigation."

4.5 CAPTURING OF SOCIAL MEDIA EVIDENCE – LEGAL CONSIDERATIONS

Social media investigations can be different than many other types of investigations. In a traditional investigation involving electronic media, the investigator has some degree of control over the data, for instance, the computer data on a seized hard drive or mobile phone. However, in the realm of social media, the investigator has no control over what is happening on the "other end" of the social media site in question (Lillard, Garrison, Schiller, & Steele, 2010). This can be a legal red-flag from the perspective that just like traditional evidence, social media evidence must be collected in a controlled and proper forensic manner. This difficulty is further complicated by the nonavailability and lack of court-validated digital forensic tools that are available for the collection and analysis of social media evidence. The use of freeware and/or shareware capturing utilities or tools for capturing evidence from social media sites, absent consideration of the legal implications and ramifications that may arise, must be resisted in the light of recent case law indicating that courts are applying increasingly stringent requirements for admissibility where social media evidence is involved (Brunty, 2011). With that said, in order to provide social media evidence that can withstand intense legal scrutiny, we must look at the relevant case law and legal baselines that currently exist.

Capturing and collecting social media data in a legally reasonable and court-accepted form should be guided by the current rules of evidence that exist in the legal community. In the United States, the US Federal Rules of Evidence is the legal measuring stick for any form of electronic evidence, including social media evidence. The Federal Rules of Evidence covers both civil and criminal evidence with some rules applying directly to one or the other. One of the provisions that can be directly applied to the capture and collection of online social media evidence is that of Rule 1001, which refers to the contents of writings, recordings and photographs. This rules generally requires the original or reliable duplicate of any *"writing, recording or photograph"* when the content of that evidence is given legal significance by substantive law (such as a copyrighted picture posted to a social media site) or by the parties themselves (such as using a video recording posted to a social media site of a particular crime). This is commonly referred to as the "Best Evidence Rule" which in short limits the admissibility of evidence to merely the best that the nature of the case will allow (Garrison, 2010). To exemplify, it can be implied that an original online posting of a particular Facebook profile can essentially be altered by the owner of the profile at any given time, thus an effective screen capture of such evidence would suffice as the "best evidence" in place of the original.

Although there is really no *de facto* standard as to how social media artifacts should be captured legally, there are a few cases that provide precedence into how such sites can be captured. One of the more bizarre cases of collecting and capturing social media evidence comes from the case of *Barnes v. CUS Nashville*, LLC, 2010 WL 2265668 (M.D. Tenn, 2010) in which the Magistrate judge offered to create a pseudo Facebook account if two witnesses were willing to accept the magistrate judge as a "friend" on Facebook solely for the purpose of reviewing photographs and related comments *in camera-aka in chamber* (Ehrlich, 1987). After reviewing and disseminating to the parties any relevant information, the magistrate judge would close the Facebook account and issue a ruling.

There are also issues of legality that must be considered when capturing content that lies behind measures of protection such as passwords or privacy settings that prohibit accessibility to the general public. Many Facebook users do not show or broadcast their pages to the general public, but rather only to particular friends that they choose to. In many cases, only these friends can see publically available information such as posts, photos, and other content that is not readily available to the public. In August 2012, Federal Judge William Pauley ruled that accused gangster Melvin Colon is not protected by Fourth Amendment search and seizure provisions to suppress Facebook evidence that led to his indictment. According to court proceedings, Colon had argued that federal investigators had violated his privacy by accessing the information contained in his profile through an informant who happened to be one of his Facebook friends. This accessibility of Colon's profile through the informant's Facebook friendship served as a pathway into Colon's gang-related activity. Agents found that Colon had used Facebook to post about violent acts and threats to rival gangs and gang members (Roberts, 2012a). Authorities used such information to obtain a search warrant to investigate the remaining portions of Colon's Facebook account. In his issued opinion, Judge Pauley stated:

> *Where Facebook privacy settings allow viewership of postings by "friends" the Government may access them through a cooperating witness who is a "friend" without violating the fourth amendment.*
>
> **II Cr. 576 (WHP, 2012)**

A similar case involving Twitter was also brought forth which challenged the ownership and privacy of Twitter content and "tweets" in the case of *New York v. Harris* (2011-NY-080152). On October 1, 2011, the Defendant, Malcolm Harris, was charged with Disorderly Conduct after allegedly marching on the roadway of the Brooklyn Bridge as part of an Occupy Wall Street protest. On January 26, 2012, the New York District

Court sent a subpoena to Twitter seeking the defendant's account information and tweets for their relevance in the aforementioned criminal investigation. On January 30, 2012, Twitter informed the defendant that the Twitter account @destructuremal had been subpoenaed. On January 31, 2012, the defendant then notified Twitter of his intention to file a motion to quash the subpoena on the grounds that the seizure of the alleged "tweets" were protected under the Fourth Amendment. In response to the quash motion, Twitter then took the position that it would not comply with the subpoena until the court ruled on the defendant's motion to quash the subpoena and intervened. Subsequently, on April 20, 2012, the New York court held that the defendant had no proprietary interest in the user information on his Twitter account, and therefore lacked standing to quash the subpoena. In addition, the Judge ruled the defendant's Fourth Amendment rights were not violated because there was no physical intrusion of the defendant's tweets and the defendant has no reasonable expectation of privacy in the information he intentionally broadcast to the world through Twitter. Ultimately, the court ordered Twitter to provide certain information to the court as part of the original issued subpoena. In his ruling, Judge Sciarrino stated:

The Constitution gives you the right to post, but as numerous people have learned, there are still consequences for your public posts. What you give to the public belongs to the public. What you keep to yourself belongs only to you (2012).

The *Harris* ruling raises important questions about how privacy law should apply to social media as a whole. In the Harris case, Judge Sciarrino stated that Harris' tweets were ultimately Twitter's property, but also pointed out that social media sites were just like witnesses who were present on a particular street at the time a crime occurred and witnessed such activity. The Judge argued that the particular witness in that instance can be called to testify and parallels such analogy by stating that the street is an online, information superhighway, and the witnesses can be the third party providers like Twitter, Facebook, Instragram, Pinterest or the next hot social media application (Fig. 4.2) (Roberts, 2012b).

4.6 CONCLUSION

In dealing with social media issues, legal authorities such as law enforcement and judges are often asked to make decisions based on statutes and issue court opinions that can never keep up with

> **Witnesses to crime can be social media providers like Twitter, Facebook, Instragram, Pinterest, or the next hot social media application**
>
> joshbrunty, 1 minute ago

Fig. 4.2. In some cases, the only credible witness to a crime can be the content that a suspect posted to a social media site. Like a traditional witness, these social media providers can be served with a subpoena to provide information.

technology or are drafted with antiquated and/or outdated technology and technological concepts in mind. In some cases, those same law enforcement and court officials have no understanding of the social media technology in question and err in judgment and prudence when dealing with such issues. Therefore, with little or no precedence into the laws of social media existing, law enforcement must balance these issues with the precedence set forth in previous legal proceedings. The criminal justice system as a whole must then weigh the interests of society against the rights of the individual who gave away some rights created by our government and the laws that each individual has agreed to follow. While the law regarding social media is clearly still developing, it is for sure that social media has had a dramatic impact on our society and how it operates. Therefore, it is only given that such an impact will reshape our legal landscape and will continue to do so for years to come. The world of social media is evolving, as is the law around it. As the laws, rules and societal norms evolve and change with each new advance in social technology, so too will the decisions of the courts and the investigative methods and authority of law enforcement.

REFERENCES

Barnes v. CUS Nashville, LLC, 2010 WL 2265668 (M.D. Tenn. 2010).

Brandenburg v. Ohio, U.S. 444 (1969).

Brunty, J. (2011). Validation of forensic tools: A quick guide for the digital forensic examiner. *Digital Forensic Investigator (DFI) News*. Retrieved August 15, 2012 from http://www.dfinews.com/article/validation-forensic-tools-and-software-quick-guide-digital-forensic-examiner).

Ehrlich, E. (1987). *Amo, amas, amat, and more: How to use Latin to your own advantage and to the astonishment of others*. New York, NY: Harper & Row.

Gitlow v. New York, 268 U.S. 652 (1925).

Government of Dubai. (2011). *Arab social media report* (2nd ed). Retrieved August 8, 2012 from <http://www.dsg.ae/en/ASMR2/ASMRHome2.aspx?AspxAutoDetectCookieSupport=1>.

Huang, C. (2011). Facebook and Twitter key to Arab spring uprisings. *The National*. Retrieved August 8, 2012 from http://www.thenational.ae/news/uae-news/facebook-and-twitter-key-to-arab-spring-uprisings-report.

Kissing, S. (2001). Brandenburg v. Ohio. *Cincinnati Magazine*, 14–15.

Li, A. (2012). New York police subpoena twitter to identify potential Aurora shooting copycat. Retrieved August 8, 2012 from <http://mashable.com/2012/08/08/suboena-twitter-aurora>.

Lillard, T., Garrison, C., Schiller, G. and Steele, J. (2010). *Digital forensics for network, Internet, and cloud computing a forensic evidence guide for moving targets and data.* Burlington, MA: Syngress.

Maras, M. (2011). *Computer forensics: Cybercriminals, laws, and evidence.* Sudbury, MA: Jones & Bartlett.

O'Connor, M. (2012). Lawyers vow to appeal ruling that says Facebook is not "like" free speech. *Fox News.* Retrieved August 14, 2012 from <http://www.foxnews.com/politics/2012/08/14/lawyer-vows-to-appeal-runling-that-facebook-like-is-not-free-speech/>.

Ornellas v. United States, 517 U.S. 690, 696 (1996).

Petrashek, N. (2010). The fourth amendment and the brave new world of online social networking. *Harvard Law Review, 93*(4) Marquette: Marquette Press.

Roberts, J. (2012a). "Friends" can share your Facebook profile with the government, court rules. *GigaOM.* Retrieved August 15, 2012 from <http://gigaom.com/2012/08/15/friends-can-share-your-facebook-profile-with-the-government-court-rules>.

Roberts, J. (2012b). Social media judge says tweets are for cops. *GigaOM.* Retrieved July 3, 2012 from <http://gigaom.com/2012/07/02/social-media-judge-says-tweets-are-for-cops/>.

Ruderman, W. (2012). Court prompts Twitter to give data to police in threat case. *The New York Times.* Retrieved August 7, 2012 from <http://www.nytimes.com/2012/08/08/nyregion/after-court-order-twitter-sends-data-on-user-issuing-threats.html?_r=3&nl=todaysheadlines&emc=edit_th_20120808>.

Schenck v. the United States, 249 U.S. 47 (1919).

State of New York v. Harris, 2012 NY Slip Op 22175 (2011).

U.S. Const. amend. I. Retrieved August 10, 2012 from <http://www.archives.gov/exhibits/charters/bill_of_rights_transcript.html>.

U.S. Const. amend. IV. Retrieved August 10, 2012 from <http://www.archives.gov/exhibits/charters/bill_of_rights_transcript.html>.

Vergakis, B. (2012). Facebook "like" button is protected speech. *San Francisco Chronicle.* Retrieved August 8, 2012 from <http://www.sfgate.com/news/article/Facebook-Like-button-is-protected-speech-3771892.php#ixzz24Icz8vR2>.

CHAPTER 5

Moving Forward

5.1 INVESTIGATIVE/INTELLIGENCE CHANGES

Some law enforcement agencies are already relying on social media sites as a tool to aid in the monitoring of known groups, gangs and criminals. As more agencies discover the valuable information that can be found on media sites, they will turn to the Internet to help perform investigations. Units may look into the hiring and training officers to learn the ropes of social media and work purely online instead of in the field.

As mobile technologies and "cloud"-based resources continue to gain popularity in mainstream society, so will usage of social media. Operating systems such as Microsoft (Windows) and Apple (OS/X & iOS) have integrated social media applications like Twitter and Facebook into their most recent releases, further increasing the amount of potential residual evidence left behind on a particular suspect machine or device and on the network. The integration of these so-called "apps" will further propagate social media usage among the general population base.

In addition, the national and international intelligence communities will increasingly look at social media sites as a method to monitor potential and established terrorist networks, both domestic and abroad. It was discovered in September 2012 that Taliban insurgents in Afghanistan had created fake Facebook accounts posing as "attractive women" to befriend coalition soldiers (United States, Australia, Great Britain) in order to gain intelligence such as military strategy and positioning, and other data-mined information such as geotagged photos (Deceglie and Robertson, 2012).

As both technology and the end-users of social media become accustomed to a globally interconnected network, the investigators tasked with enforcing and investigating the presence of criminal activity within this global network will change and morph drastically in the upcoming years, if not months, ahead.

5.2 MONITORING OF CRIMINAL ACTIVITY VIA SOCIAL MEDIA

Just as social media sites keep growing and expanding, their use by individuals will grow and expand as well. This not only means for personal and business use but also for criminal and terrorist use as well. Criminals understand and take advantage of the easy accessibility that so many social media sites offer. Observing and examining activities online could help solve cold cases and open investigations. The activities online may actually be malicious in and of themselves.

As social media continues to propagate "tweets," "status updates" and photos, the interest of law enforcement to data-mine and monitor such information is becoming increasingly popular. As a result, software developers are beginning to progress applications to capture and parse such massive amounts of publically available information, a concept loosely referred to as "dataveillance." Acting much like search engines, these applications will allow easy aggregation and allow effective searching of massive web-based databases. It is estimated that a large portion of the web is invisible, nearly 60 to 80%. This is known as the "invisible web" or the "deep web" and is mainly the underlying databases, content and object and event-driven code that drives the front-end content that we see in our everyday activity on the computer screen; some of this underlying information may be of relevance to a particular investigation. In addition, the collection of such data can provide effective intelligence into users or groups of interest.

5.3 FUTURE LEGISLATION

Each day, new interpretations of the law regarding social media use are being established. One analysis and explanation of the law may become completely turned around and the opposite may be true the next day. With the new technology and issues that are appearing each day, the courts are attempting to catch up and stay as recent as possible; this can be difficult, though, with all of the crimes, freedom of speech rights, and search and seizure issues being brought into question. New legislation is being accepted and preceding law is still being interpreted as best as possible and is subject to change each day.

The groundwork for new legislation is being set in place in such issues as social media privacy and expectation of privacy, cyberbullying and overall freedom of speech regarding online content. Legislation such as the Stored Communications Act (SCA) is relatively antiquated when it comes to the issue of social media and its underlying issues. With the proliferation of social media and its potential negative backlashes from a political perspective in mainstream media, legislators will ultimately place social media to the top of the list of proposed future legislation.

5.4 NEGATIVE EFFECTS OF SOCIAL MEDIA

Social media infiltrates the lives of its members – it is available at any hour of the day on any device that has Internet capabilities. This characteristic of social media certainly has some positive effects; but, as addressed in previous chapters, many negative outcomes can occur from the constant availability these sites offer. Online taunting and harassment do not just stop when one decides to go to sleep. Cyberterrorists do not stop planning just because it is after work hours. Identity thieves can steal personal information at any hour of the night – the availability of social sites is always constant.

Many servers and Internet Service Providers are located not only all across the United States but also throughout the world. Furthermore, information located in the cloud, which is available to many users, is under debate about whether this data can freely be grabbed and used by law enforcement. When it comes to preparing subpoenas, court orders and warrants, there are certain issues that can arise when crossing state lines or national boundaries. Some perpetrators realize this and will purposely send information to servers in other countries and then back to where it originated from to confuse law enforcement. Opposing opinions regarding the acquisition of data sparks debate as to whether states should freely cooperate with one another regarding Internet evidence, or if the typical measures of attempting to obtain data from an Internet Service Provider in a different state should be kept as is.

5.5 PROLIFERATION OF SOCIAL MEDIA

Social media continues to grow and expand; sites give users a way to feel connected to the world. They create a community where like-minded people can meet and discuss their thoughts and ideas. Members are able to share their opinions and have them posted on national news. They can talk with celebrities and be on the front line for the latest issues. New social media sites will surface and popular social media sites will continue to spread with new and innovative tools.

Another problem causing possible issues for law enforcement is the extreme amount of information and data that is on social media sites. Many forensic laboratories, digital laboratories included, already have a current backlog. Attempting to comb through social media sites and post for specific entries could become an extremely time-consuming process for investigators. Certain forensic software is specifically designed to aid in the search for Internet and social media artifacts; however, the immense quantity of data still takes time for investigators to sort through.

5.6 CHALLENGES THAT LIE AHEAD

A huge question that will continue to be asked is "Who is responsible for what happens on the Internet?" When a teen commits suicide from cyberbullying, who is responsible? When someone posts a webpage about murdering someone and it is made available by an Internet Service Provider, who is responsible? Where is the line drawn? There have been attempts made to pass legislation making Internet users as culpable for their actions in cyberspace as they would be in the physical world.

Keeping the legislation and laws as up to date as the social media technology has proven to be an issue. Attempting to apply old laws to new technology can be difficult and problematic. Furthermore, the first amendment issue of free speech and the fourth amendment regarding search and seizure as they apply to the Internet will continue to be under debate.

5.7 CONCLUSION

Hopefully this book has opened your eyes and minds to the malicious uses of social media and the potential benefits these sites holds for law enforcement. There are constantly new ways to think outside of the box when it comes to using these social sites – whether for common purposes, criminal uses and law enforcement investigations. Make sure to stay aware of new security issues and novel legal decisions that may impact social media use. This is an area that changes every day and will affect each and every Internet user.

REFERENCE

Deceglie, A., and Robertson, K. (2012, September 9). Taliban using Facebook to lure Aussie soldier. *News.com.au.* Retrieved September 9, 2012, from <http://www.news.com.au/national/taliban-using-facebook-to-lure-aussie-soldier/story-fndo4bst-1226468094586>.

Sample Social Media Preservation Letter Request

[Social Media Service Provider]
[Address]
[City, State, ZIP]

VIA FAX to (xxx) xxx-xxxx

Dear:

I am writing to [*confirm our telephone conversation earlier today and to*] make a formal request for the preservation of records and other evidence pursuant to 18 U.S.C. § 2703(f) pending further legal process.

You are hereby requested to preserve, for a period of ninety (90) days, the records described below currently in your possession, including records stored on backup media, in a form that includes the complete record. You also are requested not to disclose the existence of this request to the subscriber or any other person, other than as necessary to comply with this request. If compliance with this request may result in a permanent or temporary termination of service to the accounts described below, or otherwise alert the subscriber or user of these accounts as to your actions to preserve the referenced files and records, please contact me before taking such actions.

This request applies only retrospectively. It does not in any way obligate you, nor are you being asked, to capture and preserve new information that arises after the date of this request.

This preservation request applies to the following records and evidence:

A. All stored communications and other files reflecting communications to or from [Social Media Account User Name (between DATE1 at TIME1 and DATE2 at TIME2)];

B. All files that have been accessed by [Social Media Account/User Name (between DATE1 at TIME1 and DATE2 at TIME2)] or are controlled by user accounts associated with [Social Media Account User Name (between DATE1 at TIME1 and DATE2 at TIME2)];

C. All connection logs and records of user activity for [Social Media Account User Name (between DATE1 at TIME1 and DATE2 at TIME2)], including:

1. Connection date and time;
2. Disconnect date and time;
3. Method of connection (e.g., Telnet, ftp, http);
4. Type of connection (e.g., modem, cable/DSL, T1/LAN);
5. Data transfer volume;
6. User name associated with the connection and other connection information, including the Internet Protocol address of the source of the connection;
7. Communication records;
8. Records of files or system attributes accessed, modified or added by the user;
9. Connection information for other computers to which the user of the [Social Media Account User Name (between DATE1 at TIME1 and DATE2 at TIME2)] connected, by any means, during the connection period, including the destination IP address, connection time and date, disconnect time and date, method of connection to the destination computer, the identities (account and screen names) and subscriber information, if known, for any person or entity to which such connection information relates, and all other information related to the connection from ISP or its subsidiaries.
10. All records and other evidence relating to the subscriber(s), customer(s), account holder(s), or other entity(ies) associated with [Social Media Account User Name] (between DATE1 at TIME1 and DATE2 at TIME2)], including, without limitation, subscriber names, user names, screen names or other identities, mailing addresses, residential addresses, business addresses, e-mail addresses and other contact information, telephone numbers or other subscriber number or identifier number, billing records, information about the length of service and the types of services the subscriber or customer utilized and any other identifying information, whether such records or other evidence are in electronic or other form.

Any other records and other evidence relating to [Social Media Account User Name (between DATE1 at TIME1 and DATE2 at

TIME2)]. Such records and other evidence include, without limitation, correspondence and other records of contact by any person or entity about the above-referenced account, the content and connection logs associated with or relating to postings, and communications and any other activities to or through [Social Media Account User name] (between DATE1 at TIME1 and DATE2 at TIME2)], whether such records or other evidence are in electronic or other form.

Very truly yours,

Signature _____

Printed Name _____

Title_____

Badge/ID Number_____

Sample Social Media Subpoena Request

IN THE CIRCUIT COURT IN AND FOR <u>COUNTY</u>, <u>STATE</u>

IN RE: STATEWIDE PROSECUTOR: WVMU No.: 2012–0091–001
CRIMINAL INVESTIGATION: Subpoena No.: 12–123

INVESTIGATIVE SUBPOENA DUCES TECUM

IN THE NAME OF THE STATE OF _____, TO ALL AND
SINGULAR THE AGENTS OF THE _____ DEPARTMENT
OF PUBLIC SAFETY AND/OR THE SHERIFFS OF THE STATE
OF _____.

YOU ARE COMMANDED TO SUMMON:

Social Media Service Provider
Attn:_____
Address
City, State Zip Code

to appear before the undersigned Prosecutor on the ___ day of _____,
2012 at 1 p.m. at the Office of the Prosecutor, 123 Fake Street.,
Faketown, WV, 12345, to testify truthfully in behalf of the State of
_____, and to bring with her the following items:

**Please provide us with the information of [Social Media User ID or
Username] including:**
name, length of service, credit card information, e-mail address(es)
and a recent login IP address of social media account as defined in
18 U.S.C. Section 2703(c)(2).

This SUBPOENA is issued under the authority of the Circuit Court, at
the request of the Office of the Prosecutor, by and through the undersigned prosecuting attorney. Failure to obey this Order may be pun-
ished as contempt of court.

In lieu of personal appearance, these items may be furnished on or before the above date by **mail or personal delivery to:**

Prosecutor Name
Prosecutor Title (e.g. County or State Prosecutor)
123 Fake Street
Faketown, WV, 12345

This subpoena is issued as part of an ongoing criminal investigation. Do not disclose the existence of this subpoena or the State's investigation to (YOUR CUSTOMERS, SUBSCRIBERS, ETC.).

IN WITNESS WHEREOF, I have set my hand hereunto, and the seal of the Court at City Name, State name, this_____day of September, 2012.

_____

CLERK OF THE COURT

BY: _____ (Seal)
Deputy Clerk-Clerk of the Circuit Court

BY:

Prosecutor Name
Prosecutor Title (e.g. County or State Prosecutor)
123 Fake Street
Faketown, WV, 12345

Personally served this _____ day of September, 2012

By: _____

In accordance with the Americans With Disabilities Act, persons with a disability who need special accommodations to participate in this proceeding should contact _____, Prosecuting Attorney, not later than ten (10) days prior to the proceeding.

Sample Social Media Court Order

**IN THE CIRCUIT COURT OF _____ COUNTY,
WEST VIRGINIA**

STATE OF WEST VIRGINIA,

V.

PRIOR TO ACTION OF THE GRAND JURY INVESTIGATION

ORDER

Came this day the State of West Virginia by Prosecuting Attorney, _____, and requested this Court for an Order directing **SOCIAL MEDIA ACCOUNT PROVIDER, 450 DEAD END ROAD, FAKETOWN, WEST VIRGINIA. 08057, PHONE: (123)-456-7890, FAX: (987)-654-3210**, to provide to _____ of the _____ Police Dept., subscriber information associated with the use of the below listed [Social Media ID Number or Username] on the specified dates, which shall be used in an ongoing criminal investigation; and directing **SOCIAL MEDIA ACCOUNT PROVIDER, 450 DEAD END ROAD, FAKETOWN, WEST VIRGINIA. 08057, PHONE: (123)-456-7890, FAX: (987)-654-3210**, to delay notice of the execution of any such Order to any customer(s) or subscriber(s) for period of Ninety (90) days from the date of the execution of any said Order, in that any immediate notice of any such Order may have an adverse result which would seriously jeopardize the on-going investigation or cause the destruction of or tampering with any evidence.

The court compels the disclosure of stored contents of the aforementioned social media account. The Court is addressed and hereby finds, that the purpose of such information is to locate computers reasonably believed, based on this investigation, to be involved in felony identity theft; that such information is necessary and can be obtained from no other source and that any privacy interests are outweighed by the legitimate law enforcement need for such information.

WHEREFORE this Court, having considered the foregoing, hereby **ORDERS** as follows:

1. **SOCIAL MEDIA ACCOUNT SERVICE PROVIDER, 450 DEAD END ROAD, FAKETOWN, WEST VIRGINIA. 08057, PHONE: (123)-456-7890, FAX: (987)-654-3210**, shall furnish to Officer _____ of the _____ Police Dept, 1401 Forensic Science Drive, Huntington, West Virginia. 25701, information associated with the use of the above listed [Social Media ID Number or Username] that was utilized on the date and time specified above.

2. Said basic subscriber information shall include:
   a. All names of persons listed on any such accounts;
   b. All addresses listed on any such accounts;
   c. Records of session times and durations;
   d. Recent login IP addresses
   e. The length of service, including start date, and types of service utilized;
   f. Message headers and IP addresses
   g. The means and source of payment for such service, including any credit card or bank account number.
   h. E-mail addresses associated with the accounts

3. **SOCIAL MEDIA ACCOUNT PROVIDER, 450 DEAD END ROAD, FAKETOWN, NEW JERSEY. 08057, PHONE: (123)-456-7890, FAX: (987)-654-3210**, shall delay any required notice, if any, of the execution of this Order to any customer(s) or subscriber(s) for period of Ninety (90) days from the date of the execution of this Order.

4. The Clerk of this Court shall forward a certified copy of this Order to Officer _____ of the _____ Police Dept. for service to **SOCIAL MEDIA ACCOUNT PROVIDER, 450 DEAD END ROAD, FAKETOWN, WEST VIRGINIA. 08057, PHONE: (123)-456-7890, FAX: (987)-654-3210**

All of which is hereby **ORDERED** this _____ day of_____, 2012.

ENTERED:

_____
CIRCUIT COURT JUDGE

APPROVED BY:_____

Media Emergency Disclosure Request Form

Agency Name:
Investigator Name:
Investigator Badge #:
Requesting Investigator work-authorized e-mail:
Requesting Investigator phone number including any extension:

In this paragraph, provide a detailed description of the nature of the emergency (i.e., potential bodily harm, crime being committed, danger to child, etc.):

In this paragraph, provide identifying Information for user account (Social Media Account ID):Detailed explanation of information needed to resolve emergency:

I,_____ attest that the above-mentioned facts are true and accurate to the best of my knowledge.

Signature and Badge #:_____

Date:_____

Made in the USA
San Bernardino, CA
30 January 2016